Women Elders
In The Kirk?

Edited By
Rev. Dr. A. T. B. McGowan

Christian Focus Publications Ltd.

© Christian Focus Publications Ltd.

ISBN 1 871676 304

Published by
Christian Focus Publications Ltd.
Geanies House, Fearn, Ross-shire,
IV20 1TW, Scotland, Great Britain.

Contents

Page

Notes on Contributors

The Rev. Dr. Andrew T.B. McGowan (Editor)
Andrew McGowan is Minister of Trinity Possil & Henry
Drummond Church in Glasgow. He is a Director of the
Bible Training Institute in Glasgow and a member of the
Council of Rutherford House in Edinburgh. He
contributed to the volume *Man, Woman and Priesthood*
(Gracewing, 1989), a symposium on women's ordination,
and was the author of the 1989/90 issue of *Pray Today*
published by the Church of Scotland.

The Rev. Ian Hamilton
Ian Hamilton is Minister of Loudoun Church in
Newmilns. He is a member of the Council of Rutherford
House. His M.Phil. thesis, *The Erosion of Calvinist
Orthodoxy*, has just been published in the *Rutherford
Studies in Historical Theology* series.

The Rev. C. Peter White
Peter White is Principal of the Bible Training Institute,
Glasgow. He was previously a parish minister in
Edinburgh for 16 years. He is a former secretary of the
Scottish Tyndale Fellowship for Biblical Research. He
has written a number of articles in various theological
journals as well as writing a First Communicants' course
soon to be published by Rutherford House.

The Rev. David A. Young
David Young is Minister of Kirkmuirhill Parish Church
where he has served for the past 16 years. A former
Moderator of the Presbytery of Lanark, he is currently the
Convener of its Business Committee. He contributed a
chapter to *Local Church Evangelism* (St Andrew Press,
1987).

INTRODUCTION

Setting the Scene

The ordination of women is an issue which is currently causing major problems in the Church of England. The matter has recently been further complicated by the ordination of women priests in Churches which belong to the Anglican communion. There appears to be a very real danger that the Church of England could split unless a satisfactory solution is reached.

The Church of Scotland, on the other hand, has had women ordained to the ministry and the eldership for almost a quarter of a century. Despite this, however, the issue of women's ordination is beginning to cause difficulties and to provoke discussion within the Kirk.

The purpose of this book is twofold. On a theological level, the intention is to contribute to this important, ongoing debate. On a practical level, the intention is to help avoid an unnecessary confrontation on the issue.

Women Elders in the Kirk?

Confrontation?

It might be thought that, far from avoiding confrontation, this book might actually provoke it! That would be most unfortunate. By raising the subject quietly and openly, outwith the flames of controversy and media attention which almost always accompany a 'case' at the General Assembly, we hope that the issues involved can be explored in a relatively calm and thoughtful atmosphere.

There is no doubt that the possibility of a 'case' exists. In other words, it is quite possible to conceive of a situation where a minister might be deposed for refusing to participate in the ordination of a woman. Such a situation almost arose recently, as we shall see in a later chapter.

It is our sincere hope and prayer that this book may help to avoid such a situation, by drawing attention to some of the issues which concern us, and by suggesting some ways in which the situation might be handled by the Church of Scotland.

Different Opinions

Perhaps the first thing to stress is that this is not a simple matter. There are many different opinions on the subject of women's ordination, and even within the two main camps ('for' and 'against') there can be a variety of reasons for the position taken.

In the Church of England, for example, the opponents of women's ordination are divided into a number of groups: there are the Anglo-Catholics who do not believe that a woman can represent Christ at the Table as a priest; there are those who oppose women's ordination because of their understanding of Church history or Church tradition; there are those who are concerned that such a move would prevent reunion with the Roman Catholic Church; there are the evangelicals who are against it for biblical reasons; there are those who believe that a woman can be part of a team but not a team leader; and so on.

In the Church of Scotland, most of those who do not agree with the ordination of women are in the evangelical wing of the Church. But there is no clear unanimity of view even within that broad grouping. At least three different positions are held:

1.   Those like the Rev. Dr. Angus Stewart who believe that women can and may be ordained, and who suggest that the teaching of the Bible when properly understood and explained leads to that conclusion. [1]

2.   Those like the Rev. Dr. Nigel Cameron who believe that women ought not to be ordained, but who believe that in the last analysis evangelicals ought to ordain women because of the law of the Church. [2]

3.   Those like myself who believe that the Bible does not permit the ordination of women and who therefore would not participate in such ordinations.

Add to this the many different views which exist in the rest of the Church, both for and against women's ordination, and it can immediately be seen that this is a highly complex and sensitive area of debate, and one which requires both honesty and mutual respect.

Those who argue that the issue is settled and ought not to be raised again are failing to take seriously both the current debate within the Church worldwide, and the diversity of opinion which exists in the Church of Scotland even after twenty five years.

Outline of Contents

Much has been said and written in favour of women's ordination, and that obviously is the status quo within the Church. Our contribution to the debate comes from the other side.

As evangelicals, our principal concern is with the Bible. Ian Hamilton begins our symposium by outlining the view that we have of the Bible, and reflecting theologically on the relevance of this doctrine of Scripture for the subject of women's ordination.

Ian having argued that the Bible is the revealed Word of God, and that the life of the Church must be governed by its teaching, including what we say about the ordination of women, Peter White then presents us with a careful and painstaking analysis of all the relevant biblical material.

In the next chapter I try to demonstrate that the Church of Scotland has changed its position on the issue of women's ordination. Originally 'permitting' the ordination of women, many seem now to be 'demanding' it, and putting pressure upon those who will not participate.

David Young takes up the subject of conscience and its relation to Church law and explores it in some detail, particularly the practical issue of what we ought to do when these come into conflict. He gives a useful assessment of the problems and options facing ministers who feel unable to participate in the ordination of women.

In the conclusion some of the threads of the argument are drawn together and some suggestions offered for the way ahead.

It must be emphasised that each writer is responsible only for his own contribution. This is a symposium rather than a composite work, and there are minor points at which we would disagree with one another, either in content or in form of expression. Having said that, however, I would want to stress that we are in fundamental agreement on the basic points at issue, namely, that women ought not to be ordained to the eldership (teaching or ruling) in the Church of Scotland, and that ministers who share this view ought not to be penalised by the courts of the Church.

There are also a few points at which overlap occurs between the chapters. That is an inevitable fact when engaged in this type of book. Much of the overlap has been edited out, but some necessarily remains.

Women Elders in the Kirk?

Objective

I have been asked several times recently what the purpose of the book is, and what our objectives are.

This is a difficult question to answer since we are not unaware of the level of the difficulties which face us. There are relatively few congregations which do not have women elders, and the Church of Scotland will not easily be persuaded that it was a mistake to ordain women. As realists we would recognise that our chances of turning the tide are not dissimilar to those of Canute!

This does not mean, however, that we go into battle with defeat in mind. Rather it means that we are sufficiently pragmatic to aim for limited objectives as a first stage. In particular, we are very concerned that first, no minister should be forced to act against his conscience; second, that no minister should be deposed because of his views on this issue; and third, that no candidate for ordination should be turned down because he is opposed to women's ordination. These, I believe, are realisable objectives.

Debate

Above all, however, we want to promote debate, and to ask that our position be taken seriously and given the respect it deserves. I find it rather strange that some of those who displayed righteous indignation in the 'Lord Mackay' case are dismissive of our position. The issue at stake with Lord Mackay was whether or not he was entitled to freedom of conscience. Having criticised the Free Presbyterian Church for trying to take away Lord Mackay's freedom of conscience, should the Church of Scotland remove ours?

Professor Donald MacLeod, writing about freedom of conscience and the respective authority of the Bible and the General Assembly says this,

> 'We are very close to a presbyterian magisterium, whereby the General Assembly not only issues authoritative pronouncements as to the meaning of Scripture but even presumes to decide which parts of the canon are canonical. Desperate to escape from a fundamentalist view of the Bible the Kirk has landed in a fundamentalist view of the General Assembly; and we find ourselves bound by the doctrines and commandments of men, even when they are blatantly unscriptural. We have neither Polish Pope nor paper Pope. Instead we have an infallible ballot-box: God correcting the mistakes of his apostles by means of a majority of the votes cast in the General Assembly.' [3]

Conclusion

Lest it be thought that we do not accept the authority of the Church, or are in breach of our ordination vows, it must be said in closing that we are all ministers in the Church of Scotland, and we play a full part in the life and work of the Church, both in the presbyteries to which we belong, and in General Assemblies at which we have been present. We are

Presbyterians and recognise the law of the Church. This does not imply, however, an implicit obedience irrespective of conscience. It is a conditional obedience. The four men involved in the First Secession (1733), in one of their representations, gave it as their opinion that the established Church had departed from Reformed principles, and hence they must disobey. They wrote,

> 'We are indeed bound, at our ordination, to subject ourselves unto the judicatories of the Church; but it is not an absolute subjection that we engage unto: It is not a blind and implicit obedience that we bind ourselves unto, but a subjection in the Lord; a subjection qualified and limited by the word of God, and the received and known principles of this Church.' [4]

That is our position, and we fervently hope that the Church of Scotland will recognise it to be an honourable and acceptable position both for us and for others. If that is accomplished then this book will have served a useful purpose.

A. T. B. McGowan (Editor)

NOTES
1. See Dr Stewart's article in *Life & Work*, January 1990, p.17.
2. See Dr Cameron's letter to *Life & Work*, February 1989.
3. Editorial in the *Free Church Monthly Record*, November, 1989.
4. Adam Gib, *The Present Truth: A Display of the Secession Testimony*, R. Fleming & A. Neill, Edinburgh, 1774, Vol.1, p.36 (note).

1

A THEOLOGICAL REFLECTION
by
Ian Hamilton

Introduction

The debate within the world-wide Church concerning the ordination of women is not a recent development. The present century has seen an increasing concern for the 'rights' of women in society as a whole. The clamour and demand for women to be accorded equal eligibility with men for office in the Church, has arisen out of the more general concern to 'dignify' womanhood. It can hardly be denied that for far too long women in general have been forced to play second fiddle to men, both within the Church and outside it. There is much, therefore, that Christians welcome, or should welcome, in the concern to give the role of women in society and in the Church the dignity the Word of God gives them. The Bible unequivocably asserts the equal dignity and value of men and women. Both are made 'in the image of God'.[1] When women are, therefore, relegated exclusively to the kitchen, and occupy an exclusively female sub-culture within the Church, we are introducing into the Church of God a male chauvinism that is an affront to God and a denial of

13

the dignity and ministry the Scriptures accord to women.

While Christians should welcome every effort to assert the equal dignity and value of men and women, we must never lose sight of the fact that our authority in these matters is not the prevailing (and constantly changing) ideas of society, but the unchanging truth of God's Word. If necessary the Church of God must have the courage to stand against the social trends of the day when those social trends clearly contradict the revealed will of God in the Bible. One example would be the social acceptability of the practice of homosexuality. Recently an American Episcopal Bishop ordained a practicing homosexual to the ministry. To many people the Bishop is an 'enlightened' cleric. By refusing to discriminate against the practicing homosexual, the Bishop was asserting, as he claimed, the innate dignity of this man. But however much practicing homosexuality is accepted in society as an acceptable alternative to a heterosexual relationship, the Word of God could not be clearer in teaching us that such practice is contrary to God's will for his creatures and a perversion of true human relationships. [2] For Christians the issue is settled, not by the consensus of society, but by the teaching of Scripture.

Another example would be the socially acceptable practice of 'trial marriages'. No doubt 'good' reasons can be raised in support of this increasing practice; but all of them flounder beside the clear teaching of Scripture regarding the nature and permanence of marriage.[3] In such cases the Church will inevitably be castigated as 'behind the times', out of touch with life as it really is, asserting outdated convictions in an age where the only meaningful criterion is, 'If you like it, do it; if you want it, take it.' So be it! As the apostles put it, 'We must obey God rather than men.' [4]

But equally, the Church must not live and think in a time-warp. The Church may well have misunderstood or misapplied certain biblical passages over the centuries. No era, however godly, has a monopoly of the truth. We are responsible in each successive generation for thinking through the biblical traditions we have inherited, subjecting them in the light of the Holy Spirit's continuing ministry to the touchstone of Holy Scripture. As James Packer has put it, a child standing on Calvin's shoulders can see farther than Calvin. The Holy Spirit did not stop illuminating the Scriptures at the Reformation! This truth, and it is a vital truth, should be a caution to us as we face up to the claims of new insights into the truth of God's Word. The Christian is obliged to examine every 'new insight' in the light of God's Word, and not in the light of any inherited tradition, however revered.

The question of women and rule in the Church needs therefore to be approached both with an open mind and an open Bible. For the Christian the question will be settled by searching the Scriptures, not by ascertaining the prevailing consensus in society. With this in mind, any approach to this vexed and controversial question will be governed by two principles: First, that Scripture is the Christian's only rule of faith and practice; and secondly, that it can never be right to violate our Scripture-taught conscience.

Scripture: The Christian's only Rule of Faith & Practice

The issue that pre-eminently confronts us as we grapple with the controversial question of women's ordination is that of the authority of Scripture. To those who accept the Bible as 'God-breathed', the wholly true and authoritative Word of God, the issue will be resolved by ascertaining what the Scriptures teach on this matter. If we accept that Scripture forbids women from exercising rule in the Church (as Peter White has endeavoured to show in his chapter), the issue for the Christian is resolved. God has spoken. And whatever God has spoken the Christian is bound, gladly, to believe and obey.

Until recent years, evangelicals have stood by this statement in the Westminster Confession of Faith: 'The Supreme Judge, by which all controversies of religion are to be determined, and all decrees of councils, opinions of ancient writers, doctrines of men, and private spirits, are to be examined, and in whose sentence we are to rest, can be no other but the Holy Spirit speaking in the scripture.' [5]

It seems, however, that many evangelicals no longer believe that Scripture must always be obeyed. One of the features of the general evangelical response to the pressure for women's ordination has been a reluctance to stand by the scriptural teaching regarding this issue. This reluctance by and large stems from one of two convictions. Some do not see the issue as being important enough to justify their opposition to the present law of the Church. Others are so committed to the denomination that they are ready to accept women's ordination (albeit reluctantly), rather than risk being ejected from the Church, or risk becoming marginalised within the Church. They see no alternative to the Church of Scotland and will, therefore, do what has to be done to remain within the Church.

In order to judge on the rightness of such a position we are bound to ask whether we ever have the right to set aside the teaching of God's Word for any reason. Are there occasions when it is proper to acknowledge the teaching of God's Word, and then put it to one side to accommodate contrary opinions? Do we ever have the right not to practise unqualified obedience to Holy Scripture?

There would seem to be a simple answer to these weighty questions. The authority of God's Word is set before us not merely as a doctrine to subscribe, but as a reality to live by. Our Lord did not say, "Blessed are those who hear the word of God", but "Blessed are those who hear the word of God and

Women Elders in the Kirk?

obey it".[6] For the evangelical the controlling principle in life is not the prevailing views of society, nor the accepted opinions currently in fashion within denominations, but the mind of God revealed in the Scriptures. This controlling principle may seem naive to some and not in touch with the harsh realities of living in a fallen world to others; but it is the revealed basis of living a God-honouring life.

More to the point, it has been suggested that this 'simplistic' view does not take into account the complex and complicated realities existing within mainstream denominations. We are told that it is impossible to minister within or be part of these denominations unless we learn to accomodate our biblical convictions when 'need' arises. There is a certain cogency of thought behind this view. The argument goes that if we persist in pursuing biblical convictions regardless of the denomination's canon law, refusing to practise what we believe Scripture opposes, we face either being relegated to the Church's margins, spiritually and geographically, or being removed from the Church for contumacy. Either scenario would rob the Church of evangelical influence and leave it at the mercy of liberalism.

This argument, which purports to have the best interests of the Church at heart, is in fact a recipe for disaster. When Peter and John and the other Apostles were ordered by the Sanhedrin to leave off preaching in the name of Jesus, their response has been preserved for us in Scripture for our instruction and encouragement:

'Judge for yourselves whether it is right in God's sight to obey you rather than God.'

'We must obey God rather than man!' [7]

The fundamental principle being enshrined for us in these words is that the Christian's first loyalty is to his Lord and his Word, not to any ecclesiastical assembly, however ancient and respected. Where Scripture is clear and unambiguous, where the Word of God commands, the Christian has but one option: Here I stand, I can do no other! Such an attitude may well be thought extreme, tendentious, and a recipe for provoking violent reaction. It certainly did not make life easy for the Apostles. But what else can a consistent Christian do?

Scripture is not to be picked up and put down depending on the prevailing ecclesiastical opinion. It is the Christian's only rule of faith and life at all times. The moment it is departed from the Church becomes hostage to the changing opinions of men, and places itself outwith the orbit of God's blessing. God will never bless disobedience, especially the disobedience that is calculated. Is not the history of the Church full of examples of men and women who put truth before consequences and lived to see God honour their faithfulness? The courage and uncompromising steadfastness of the Apostles, Athanasius, Luther, Calvin, Knox, and a host of more modern saints, are etched in history not merely for our admiration but also our emulation.

Women Elders in the Kirk?

The concern of those who advocate a policy of accommodation to the Church's law on the ordination of women, that they are determined to preserve an evangelical witness in the Church at all costs, must also be faced. The desire to maintain an evangelical testimony within the Church is one that all right-thinking Christians would support. But what kind of evangelicalism would be preserved in the Church if it accommodated itself, and was seen to accommodate itself, to views that were plainly contrary to Scripture? The moment Scripture is no longer regarded in practice as the Christian's and the Church's final authority, evangelicalism becomes a virtual Pandora's box!

This is precisely what happened towards the end of the nineteenth century in the Scottish Churches. In order to maintain an evangelical witness within their denominations, many evangelicals sought to accommodate the 'new insights' afforded by Higher Criticism. This accommodation was compounded by a willingness to allow men who denied many of the fundamental doctrines of the faith to remain as ministers and professors within their respective denominations. These concessions to the prevailing ecclesiastical views of the day all but sounded the death-knell of vital Christianity within the Church of Scotland for the next two generations.

God has given us his Word to be our infallible rule in matters of faith and practice. We dare not turn aside from it, whatever the pressures. God has spoken. The Christian is bound to obey.

The Role of Conscience

The present position of the Church of Scotland allows liberty of conscience, but demands conformity of practice, in the issue of women's ordination. This is intolerable. According to the Westminster Confession of Faith, which is still the Church of Scotland's Subordinate Standard of Faith, Christians are obligated to uphold the lawful authority of the Church. The Confession also acknowledges, however, the fallibility of ecclesiastical courts, and allows for liberty of conscience in matters that are either contrary to Scripture or not clearly commanded in Scripture.

'God alone is Lord of the conscience, and hath left it free from the doctrines and commandments of men which are in anything contrary to his word, or beside it, in matters of faith or worship. So that to believe such doctrines, or to obey such commandments out of conscience, is to betray true liberty of conscience.'[8]

The Confession is simply echoing Calvin's teaching in its insistence that it can never be right to act contrary to conscience. In his Commentary on 1 Corinthians, Calvin maintains that,

'God does not want us to set our hand to anything without being quite sure that it is acceptable to him. Therefore, anything a person does with a wavering conscience is, because of that very uncertainty, sinful in God's sight... Therefore let us remember that we are rushing headlong to disaster whenever we persist in our own way in opposition to our conscience.' [9]

If Calvin is fairly reflecting the biblical position, how could it be possible for evangelicals who hold to the full authority of God's Word to deny their conscience in this matter? The answer that is usually given is that the peace of the Church requires that on occasions conscientious convictions be put aside. But such thinking is to make ourselves wiser than God. The peace of the Church, that is the health and well-being of the Church, is best served by our holding to and promoting the truth of God, albeit sensitively and humbly. To sacrifice conscience in pursuit of the Church's peace is in effect to abandon the authority of Holy Scripture, the educator and definer of conscience.

The Scriptures provide us with examples of believers who were confronted by the choice of holding fast to their Scripture-taught consciences or of acquiescing in courses of action they knew to be wrong. We have already cited the example of the Apostles in Acts 4 and 5. Another striking example is Daniel. In spite of the pressures to conform to the regime in Babylon, and those who did compromise no doubt had plausible and cogent reasons for doing so, Daniel 'resolved not to defile himself with the royal food and wine'. Keil, in his Commentary on Daniel, well expresses Daniel's stand:

> 'Daniel's resolution to refrain from such unclean food flowed from fidelity to the law, and from steadfastness to the faith that "man lives not by bread only, but by every word that proceedeth out of the mouth of the Lord".' [10]

Daniel was not being extreme, he was being faithful to the revealed will of his Lord. It could have been plausibly argued that if he put his conscience in cold-storage he could have a great influence within the civil service in Babylon, and be in a position to help God's people. But Daniel put truth before consequences. Certainly Daniel was refusing to compromise with idolatry, but the principle he enacted holds for the believer whatever the circumstance: 'It is neither safe nor right to go against conscience'.

When the Church acts unlawfully by enacting legislation that is contrary to Scripture or goes beyond Scripture, the Christian cannot be bound to acquiesce in its decrees. This is not to canonise the individual's conscience. Daniel was not insisting that his conscience become the canon for other's actions, only his own. The tragedy is that the Church of Scotland seems to be insisting that every knee should bow and every tongue confess that the General Assembly's decisions must be obeyed, without a murmur of dissent. This is to bind the believer's conscience to the Church's magisterium and not to the Holy Scripture! That is medievalism.

At the Reformation the recovery of the gospel reestablished the primacy of the Scriptures in the life of the believer and the Church. One of the dangers facing us in the Kirk is the trend towards absolutising the decisions of the General Assembly. No longer is Scripture our final authority and court of appeal: that privilege lies with the General Assembly.

Those who argue that there must be occasions when conscience should be put to one side in the interests of Christian unity and the peace of the Church are surely undermining the credibility of the gospel. What ultimate credibility can we have if we are seen to violate conscience and do, or be party to, what is clearly forbidden in God's Word? Let us bring the issue down to a level that 'ordinary' Christians can readily identify with. What advice would be given to an anxious Christian under pressure to tell a lie to keep his job? There are plausible reasons why 'this once' the Christian should be advised to concede the lie: his job would be preserved (and jobs are scarce), his family would not suffer, and a 'Christian' witness would continue to be exercised in the office. This all sounds very plausible, but such advice perishes beside the clear teaching of Scripture, 'You shall not lie'. To forego conscience even 'this once', and act contrary to God's Word, could not but undermine any Christian witness.

Liberty of conscience is one of the most precious

possessions of a human being. But in asserting the fact of liberty of conscience, we are confronted by the question: What is the extent and what are the limits of this universal right of liberty of conscience?

Are there any limits at all to the right of private judgement? This is a question that demands an answer. To assert the absolute freedom of an individual to believe and act according to his or her own conscience would be a recipe for anarchy. Clearly there are bounds, as James Bannerman has put it 'beyond which freedom of conscience becomes not a right, but a wrong, and liberty degenerates into licentiousness.' [11]

Absolute liberty of conscience is limited in the first place by the teaching of Holy Scripture. Conscience and Scripture are not equal, or even co-ordinate authorities. On the contrary, conscience must always be in submission to the revealed Law of God. The first duty of conscience is to obey its Master, God. It is a commonplace of biblical religion,

> 'That liberty of conscience... which each moral and responsible being claims for himself, is not an unlimited right; it gives a man no title to believe and think and act in religious matters as he pleases, even though conscience should sanction his doing so; there is a limit to this freedom, beyond which he cannot go without sin; and that limit is the supreme enactments of God's law.' [12]

This truth has practical implications for a minister/

elder within a Kirk Session where others (even the majority) wish to ordain women (or biblically unqualified men) to the eldership. While each has the right of liberty of conscience, the fundamental issue is not the conscientious convictions of the majority, but whether those convictions are in harmony with Holy Scripture. The answer to those who argue that, in asserting our conscientious opposition to the ordination of people we believe are not eligible for rule and leadership in the Church of Christ, we are thereby denying their equally held conscientious opinion that they are eligible, is that their view is contrary to Scripture and cannot be accepted.

It must be conceded, however, that the issue is rarely as easily dealt with as that. Evangelicals are divided as to what Scripture teaches on this matter (although the vast majority in the Christian Church still believe the Scriptures do not allow us to ordain women). But, if we are persuaded that Scripture speaks clearly we are bound to obey it, irrespective of the views of others. This is clearly Paul's argument in Romans 14, which he concludes by declaring that, 'everything that does not come from faith is sin'.[13]

It is one thing to take a course of action when you are unclear as to the right course to take, and another to take a course of action knowing that it is clearly wrong to do so. The condemnation Paul speaks of in this verse, 'is not merely the condemnation of his own conscience; it is condemnation before God'.[14] We cannot avoid the biblical teaching that if a believer does what 'is not approved in his conviction and faith', he sins.

Secondly, absolute liberty of conscience is limited by the Church's authority. The Church's authority is a divinely given authority. The Westminster Confession is quick to balance liberty of conscience by relating it to the authority of the Church,

> 'They who, upon pretence of Christian liberty, shall oppose any lawful power, or the lawful exercise of it, whether it be civil or ecclesiastical, resist the ordinance of God.' [15]

It is no light thing to resist the authority of the Church, and for that reason many accept its decisions and decrees, even though they are unhappy with them. But the authority of the Church is to be a 'lawful' authority, that is, an authority that is founded upon, and declarative of, the teaching of God's Word. When the Church passes legislation that is contrary to God's Word, or goes beyond God's Word, such authority cannot be binding on the Christian's conscience.

The issue of women's ordination should not blind us to the fact that the core issue facing us is the rule and authority of God's infallible Word in the life of his Church. It is not a matter of being 'agin' women, nor of being dominated by a male chauvinism, the result of being raised in a world governed by patriarchal social structures. Our sole concern is to be faithful to God's revealed truth.

Women Elders in the Kirk?

God has called his people to a life of glad-hearted obedience. History, biblical and post-biblical, testifies that when God's people put truth and obedience above and before all other considerations, they bring glory to God, and ultimately blessing to the Church. Like Luther we must learn to cultivate the spirit that refuses to move from the only sure word in this universe, Holy Scripture; and leave the consequences (and they might well be sore and humbling) to our sovereign, all-wise, and all-loving Father.

The debate continues. Like Knox and the Scottish Reformers, our attitude and convictions should be open to persuasion. In the Preface to the Scots Confession, our reforming forefathers declared:

> 'Protestand that gif onie man will note in this our confessioun onie Artickle or sentence repugnand to Gods halie word, that it wald pleis him of his gentleness and for christian charities sake to admonish us of the same in writing; and we upon our honoures and fidelitie, be Gods grace do promise unto him satisfactioun fra the mouth of God, that is, fra his halie scriptures, or else reformation of that quhilk he sal prove to be amisse.' [16]

It would be a sad day if an open mind and a readiness to learn were ditched in favour of an entrenched traditionalism. But equally, it would be a sad day if two thousand years of Church tradition was ditched in favour of a present social consensus. The wise words of Isaiah must ever continue to be the yardstick by which Christians will examine every claimed new insight: 'To the law and the testimony! If they do not speak according to this word, they have no light of dawn.' [17]

NOTES

1. Genesis 1:26,27.
2. cf. Romans 1:24-27.
3. cf. Matthew 19:4-6.
4. Acts 5:29.
5. *Westminster Confession of Faith*, 1.10.
6. Luke 11:28.
7. Acts 4:19; 5:29.
8. *Westminster Confession of Faith*, 20.2
9. Calvin, J., *Commentary on 1st Corinthians* (Edinburgh, 1979 reprint) pp.176,179.
10. Keil, F.C., *Commentary on Daniel* (Grand Rapids, 1973 reprint) p.80
11. Bannerman, J., *The Church of Christ* (New Jersey, 1960 reprint) Vol.1, p.165.
12. ibid, p.166.
13. Romans 14:23.
14. Murray, J., *The Epistle to the Romans* (London, 1970) Vol.2 p.196.
15. *Westminster Confession of Faith*, 20.4
16. *The Scots Confession of 1560* (Edinburgh, 1937) p.41.
17. Isaiah 8:20.

2

THE BIBLICAL PICTURE
by
C. Peter White

Introduction

The Christian Church is wrestling over the issue of adequate and appropriate avenues for women's ministries. It is affecting the relationship between the Anglican and Roman Catholic Communions[1] and between the Reformed denominations in Scotland[2]. Many women feel hurt and rejected by those who hold to the Church's historic opinion on the issue. Some of those in favour of women's ordination are angered by the reluctance of those against, to implement it at Session or Presbytery level.[3] But many also are grieved as Establishment pressure is exerted, sometimes beyond the Law of the Kirk[4], against ministers who hold to the historic position.

If we are to bring about lasting healing and effective mission we must find a solution that is faithful to the gospel 'according to the Scriptures', as Wainwright observed anent the Baptismal debate[5]. This chapter, therefore, addresses the question whether the Scriptures, Christianly interpreted, allow us now to have women as well as men in positions of formal, appointed ruling and teaching authority over whole congregations. The two main views, among those who take the Biblical evidence seriously, are summarily compared in Table 1.

TABLE 1

(1) Source Text: Genesis ch.1
Historical View: Full partnership between equals.
New View: Ditto.

(2) Source Text: Genesis ch.2
Historical View: Man's headship is shown in:
(a) his primogeniture
(b) his naming woman.
New View: No male headship is implicit.

(3) Source Text: Genesis ch.3
Historical View: The Fall will distort the good, created headship for both men and women.
New View: Male headship is a result of the Fall.

(4) Source Text: General Old Testament Picture
Historical View: Women share in worship, prophecy and the lead in national life but not in headship in sacred things.
New View: Women play a full part in worship, prophecy and the lead in national life

(5) Source Text: Gospels
Historical View: Our Lord afforded women a
fresh dignity. They were the
first witnesses to his
Resurrection.
New View: Ditto.

(6) Source Text: Acts
Historical View: Women are involved in
prophecy and informal teaching.
The leadership is male.
New View: Ditto.

(7) Source Text: 1 Corinthians 7 v.34f
Historical View: No direct bearing on the issue of
women's ordination.
New View: Women should be able to serve
"fully to the Lord" therefore not
be barred from any ministry.

(8) Source Text: 1 Corinthians 11 v.3ff
Historical View: Women pray and prophesy in
worship, and are to accord man
the headship in Church as the
Son does the Father.
New View: Only applies to wives; and
"head" doesn't mean "head
over", but "source".

Women Elders in the Kirk?

(9) Source Text: 1 Corinthians 14 v. 34
Historical View: Women are excluded from a share in the ruling voice on word of prophecy, in line with Old Testament teaching.
New View: An ad hoc warning against excessive wifely chatter based on current Jewish Law. No direct bearing on the issue of women's ordination.

(10) Source Text: Galations 3 v.28
Historical View: Teaches identity of status but does not rule as to differentiation of office or function in the Church.
New view: The true spirit of Jesus. Women should be ordained to all Church office on the same basis as men.

(11) Source Text: 1 Timothy 2 v.7-15
Historical View: Forbids women having authoritative ruling/teaching office over whole congregations.
New View: An ad hoc rebuke warning wives off any domineering attitude.

(12) General   The "Gamaliel Test": God is blessing women's ministries, let us not resist God.

CONCLUSION

Historical View: Men and women are equals and both have ministries. Ruling/teaching authority in the Church is for some men only.

New View: One implication of redemption is to be rid of male headship and the exclusion of women from any work or office in the Church.

Can we decide between these two ways of undestanding God's Word? We start on the Bible's first page.

THE OLD TESTAMENT EVIDENCE
Genesis 1.26,27

'Then God said, "Let us make man in our image, in our likeness, and let them rule"... so God created man in his own image, in the image of God he created him; male and female he created them.'

The love drama has begun. The first page introduces us to the one God and his creature Man, made in his image. God is personal and plural: "let us..." The plurality is reflected in man, and in man's plurality there is differentiation: male and female. Does this reflect differentiation in God? We are not yet told.

The picture is of hearts beating as one: 'let us'...'male and female.'

Let us emphasise this perfect equality. Women and men are equal partners, needing each other for full human-ness, equally made in God's image.

This might seem obvious but the Church has not always taught in this way [6] and apparently it is still not the way many people think. Anne Atkins gives examples of chauvinism in Church life. [7] Clearly there is no place for such. The second chapter of Genesis unfolds the creation story in more detail.

Genesis 2.18-25
First there was only the man, but it was not good for him to be alone; God made a helper for him, and the man called her 'woman', for she was taken out of man.

Does Genesis 2 show Adam having any authority over Eve? The word 'helper' does not imply any. It is a word used of God when he comes to rescue those who are inadequate without him. It tells of man's incompleteness without woman and his need of help. What of Adam naming her? The text reads:

> The man said, 'This is now bone of my bones, and flesh of my flesh; she shall be called "woman", for she was taken out of man.'

P. Trible denies that this implies any authority of Adam over Eve. 'The Hebrew verb "to call",' she says, 'only connotes an establishment of power over something when it is linked with the noun "name".'[8] She finds Adam's headship in the fallen situation of Genesis 3 where Adam gives his wife the name Eve. To exercise authority is seen as part of the fallenness of the relationship between man and woman.

I see four reasons for perceiving Adam as having the authority of a firstborn in the unfallen situation of Genesis 2.

First, I can see no grounds to justify insistence that the word 'sem', name, must be present before the act of naming carries with it the implication of authority. 'The right to assign a name is the right to exercise authority.'[9] God brought Adam the animals and then the woman to see what he would call them. The two processes are couched in identical terms. The implication is that in both processes Adam is putting his God-given vicegerency into action.

Secondly, there is nothing in the text of Genesis 3 to suggest that Adam's naming his wife Eve has anything fallen about it, or that if there had been no Fall he would not have exercised this undisputed authority.

Thirdly, throughout Scripture being the firstborn implies authority and responsibility. Under Old Testament law the firstborn son received a 'double portion', became head of the family, and was responsible to look after any dependants.[10] In the New Testament, Christ is called the firstborn over creation because he has that role in relation to it.[11]

The natural 'whole Scripture' way to read of Adam's being first formed, and woman made for him [12], is to infer a similar role. The New Testament makes precisely this point out of Genesis 2.

Fourthly, this chapter deals later with the question whether 'head of' means 'head over'. At this stage we merely note that the New Testament uniformly infers Adam's headship from Genesis 2 and requires it to be applied in Church and marriage. [13]

Atkins objects to the word 'headship' on the grounds that it isn't used in Scripture. [14] The word Trinity isn't used in the Bible either but it is a useful communication tool when one is studying what the Bible teaches us about God. In the same way this chapter will use the word headship of the relationship that exists when the Bible says one party is head of another.

Genesis 3
The sorry story of the Fall is told. The serpent deceived the woman and the man followed her lead. God pronounced the sentence. Estrangement will spoil mankind's relationships: with nature beneath him, his companion beside him and God above him. Between Adam and Eve his headship will turn into dominion: 'he will rule over you.' No new element is introduced; every element is tinged with ruin.

The General Picture in the rest of the Old Testament

I have taken some of the points in this section from Hurley [15] whose balance and clarity are admirable. Israelite family life is based on the clan or 'father's house'. The father was the undisputed head in the family, the husband was in marriage. To 'ba'al' (become ruler over) a woman is to marry her [16]. Vows made by women could be revoked by their husbands or fathers but would stand if not specifically revoked [17].

We see women in leadership in the Old Testament, both informally and as judges and prophetesses. Deborah was perhaps a combination of the Queen and Margaret Thatcher in one person. As such she insisted on the nation's obedience to God as every 'godly prince' (to use Luther's phrase) should. Similarly, King Josiah consulted the prophetess Huldah when seeking a word from the Lord. [18] The role of a woman as both prophetess and wife is treated as normal and acceptable. This quite squashes the notion that there is something wrong or regrettable about having women in leadership in business and politics. John Knox's trumpet blast against the monstrous regiment (rule) of women has no justification, and Proverbs 31 should be enough to recommend to us women making a good show of business [19].

Deborah on the other hand was not, to carry the simile further, the Archbishop of Canterbury as well.

Hurley has shown convincingly that the headship in the cultus is male. [20] Not all men, however, were eligible. Only the Aaronic branch of the Levite tribe could be priests, and only other Levites their helpers. It was sacrilege for others to arrogate to themselves this role or the prerequisites that accompanied it. [21] Transgression incurred the death penalty. [22] The Law clearly distinguished between the nation's sociopolitical and religious leaders. [23]

There is no thought in the Old Testament that Levite men were more worthy, or constitutionally more suited, for their religious leadership calling; no suggestion that women, or men from other family groups, were less so. The issue was that of God's call. Hurley summarises:

> 'A principle of appointive male leadership in marriage and in public religious exercise can be discerned in the Old Testament. In civil life women met men as peers, although the marital relationship continued to apply for married women.' [24]

It remains to turn to the New Testament to see what is made of the Old Testament witness.

THE NEW TESTAMENT EVIDENCE
The Four Gospels

The openness with which Jesus spoke with women astonished even his disciples. [25] Although women were not admitted to Rabbinic schools Jesus taught them and they followed him and contributed to his support. They were prominent as witnesses to his death, burial and resurrection. Jesus appointed only male Apostles but the Gospels do not otherwise comment on the appointment of women to office within the Church. Thus Jesus as on other matters (e.g. divorce) stood quite independent of the spirit of his day. Radically he lived by and taught the picture already drawn from the opening pages of Scripture.

Acts

The opening chapters of Acts show us women playing an integral part in the life of the Church. [26] Peter's Pentecost sermon made it clear that a facet of the Kingdom is that 'your daughters' as well as 'your sons' shall prophesy; this is what happened. [27] A man and wife team took Apollos home and instructed him in the Faith. [28] There was formal office in the Church - presbyters appointed as overseers - from this early period but we are not told whether it included women. [29]

1 Corinthians 11.2-16 and 14.26-40 (esp 33b-36)

(a) 1 Corinthians 11.3. The meaning of 'head of' in the New Testament

What does 'head of' mean, in the New Testament? It has often been asserted that in Greek 'head' signifies 'source' and contains no idea of 'head over'. [30] That has some force in classical Greek. In koine Greek (the Greek of the New Testament) however, it 'denotes superior rank' [31] and in any case Paul was drawing his teaching from the Old Testament. There the word

41

head is used of the ruler of a society: 'The Lord will cut off from Israel both the head and the tail; the elders and the prominent men are the head' [32].

Jewish and early Christian literature reflect the same usage. In the Apostolic Constitutions we read, 'The bishop is head, he shouldn't give in to the tail!' In the Testament of Zebulun: 'Don't divide into two heads. For everything the Lord has made only one head. We have two shoulders, hands, feet - but all the members obey one head.' [33]

Two points come out. Headship involves being 'recognised head over', and calls for obedience to that authority. The continuity between Old Testament, Jewish and early Christian literature strongly implies that the word includes such a connotation in the New Testament. That is what we find. It has three figurative uses: as source, unitive principle and focus of authority. Care is needed to distinguish the governing thought whenever it is used. Thus in Ephesians 5.23 wives are not told 'submit because you are united' but 'submit because your husband is your head'. That this implies 'head over' follows from the combination of *hupotasso* (to rank oneself below, subject oneself) with *kephale* (head) exactly as in Ephesians 1.19. As God has subjected creation to Christ making him head over all, so wives are to submit themselves to their husbands whom God has made their head.

In 1 Corinthians 11.3 there are several reasons for

understanding *kephale* in the same way. First the parallel with Ephesians 5 is startling, based in exactly the same way on the headship of Christ. Secondly the issue at stake is that of authority. The verse is applied in the ensuing verses in terms of recognising and exercising that authority. The conclusion is irresistible that Paul sees this authority in the verse he goes on to expound. Thirdly the best parallel between all three relationships - God-Christ, Christ-man and man-woman is seen if one understands head to mean 'head over'. [34] I still have not managed to work out what people mean when they say the headship of man means only that man is source of woman in church and marriage, not that authority is invested there.

A profoundly Christological and Trinitarian pattern of headship/submission thus underlies Paul's teaching on marriage and Church relationships alike. As M.J. Williams observes, the man-woman relationship is part of the doctrines of God and the Church. [35]

But which men have what authority over which women? Paul's primary concern is that the proper relationship between husbands and wives (the Greek for woman, and for wife, is the same word) is reflected in public worship; but headship in the Church, as well as in marriage, is also at stake. Single women are not being told, however, to regard any and every male around as head over them in any way! Is Paul not saying that in marriage the husband is head over his wife, and that in the Church the oversight or presbyteral role is invested in the group of men called to it? [36]

Surely the relationships within our God himself take all the sting out of headship? Barth comments that we find the *imago dei,* the way in which man's life reflects God's, in his ability to be a partner. [37] This partnership is characterised by differentiation and relation: God always confronts himself as the Father of the Son, and vice-versa, yet always one in the Holy Spirit. The Son delights to do the Father's will, yet they are 'the same in substance, equal in power and glory'. This is the model Paul uses to set male headship in Church and marriage before us. We are now in a better position to consider the section in which 1 Corinthians 11.3 is set and applied.

(b)1 Corinthians 11.2-16
In some of its details this passage is intractably obscure. Within the uncertainties two things seem clear. First, women may exercise a speaking ministry within the life of a congregation: 'Every woman who prays or prophesies [38] with her head uncovered dishonours her head.'

Secondly, the repeated references to recognising authority and observing order must be interpreted in harmony with the basic principle enunciated in v.3. The Kirk's Panel on Doctrine agreed: the passage is mainly theological teaching rooted in Genesis 1 and 2. It teaches that man is head of woman, as Christ is of man and God of Christ. Since Roman and Greek society had women in leadership roles, Paul was not

44

merely taking account of the proprieties of his own day. Headship speaks of the other's perfect submission in love, and is quite compatible with equality between the two. Man's headship is 'in the Lord' - the distortion resulting from the Fall is healed and 'the headship of the man remains valid alongside the new equality... this is compatible with, and may require, differentiation of function'. [39]

(c) 1 Corinthians 14.33-36

The importance of understanding the Corinthian passages in harmony with their opening statement of principle is underlined when we examine 1 Corinthians 14.33-36. At first sight Paul seems to contradict part of what he has just said:

> 'As in all the congregations of the saints, women should remain silent in the churches. They are not allowed to speak, but must be in submission, as the Law says...'

May women speak (1 Cor.11) or not (1 Cor.14)? Some great commentators have assumed from chapter 14's forbiddings that the praying and prophesying of chapter 11 must have taken place in a smaller setting than the life of a Church: a home or a women's meeting. The context of 1 Corinthians 14.33b-36 however, is of a congregation evaluating a prophetic message (v.26-33). In such a case women should keep silent, Paul seems to be saying, because authority over the congregation's life is being exercised [40]: something which the Law, Genesis 2, forbids to women. (Those modern commentators who take 'The Law' here to mean contemporary Jewish law are surely wide of the mark. It would be quite extraordinary for Paul to mean anything but the Old Testament Law by this expression, used in this unqualified way.)

Galatians 3.27,28
'There is neither Jew nor Greek, slave nor free, male nor female, for you are all one in Christ Jesus.' Division and status battles are out for Christians. The passage gives no guidance as to differentiation of role or office in the Church; at about the same time the same author was writing 'respect those who are over you in the Lord' [41]. It underlines spirit and attitude in line with our Lord Jesus. [42]

Ephesians 5.21-33
These verses are not about office in the Church but the requirement of mutual submission in marriage: of husbands to sacrificial love; of wives, to 'submit to their husbands in everything.' So the teaching on headship is steadily fleshed out.

1 Peter 3.1-7
The teaching is similar to that in Ephesians. Subjection is not done away with but is a new thing in the Lord Jesus, excluding pride and self-assertiveness.

1 Timothy 2 .
Table 2 lays out the text of the core verses, 11-14, and three contemporary evangelical understandings of it. [43]

TABLE 2

1 Timothy 2.11-14 AS UNDERSTOOD BY THREE CONTEMPORARY WRITERS

Text: *A woman - in quietness let her learn with all submission*

Atkins: Let women be educated! Quietly and submissively, of course: that's the way to be a good pupil.

Baldwin: Wives are to be people of quiet assurance who can defer to others and keep their own counsel.

Hurley: I want women to learn quietly and submissively.

Text: *I do not permit a woman to teach, nor to have authority over a man, but to be in quietness (hesuchia)*

Atkins: It's not MY normal practice to use women as teachers/leaders, although I do sometimes (e.g. Priscilla & Phoebe) and what you do is up to you.

Baldwin: Married women are not to usurp absolute authority, which in any case belongs to God. No one should be domineering but it is particularly inappropiate for wives to be autocratic and in this attitude to teach (although they may rightfully be given whatever authority is appropiate to their standing in the congregation).

Hurley: I do not permit a woman to teach authoritatively; nor, indeed, to exercise other formal authority in the Church.

Text: *For Adam was formed first, then Eve. And Adam was not the one deceived; it was the woman.*

Atkins: For look what happened when Eve was not educated:... the Fall.

Hurley: (a) Adam was 'first formed': he was given an authoritative role; (b) Eve took the lead in eating the fruit. She had not been prepared for leadership and was deceived.

Certain points may best be cleared up before comparing the interpretations (I refer to the author as Paul; none of the argument is affected for readers who wish to believe otherwise).

What subject is Paul dealing with? Baldwin reckons the chapter is a general code of conduct, with specific instructions to Church leaders in chapter three. But examination of the verses leads surely to the conclusion that the subject matter is congregational life and especially public worship:

'I urge, first, that requests, prayers, intercessions and thanksgivings be made for everyone - for kings and all those in authority...'

'I do not permit a woman to teach or to have authority over a man...'

Bearing in mind that it was acceptable for women to speak publicly as long as the last instruction was not violated, and to give instruction in the home (Acts 18.26), it seems more reasonable to take it that 2.11ff deals with the relations between men and women as regards formally recognised teaching work in the Church and that chapter three then deals with the qualifications of elders and deacons. [44]

Hesuchia, quietness, does not require silence. Hurley says, 'Paul's actual words do not mean "with buttoned lips" but have the connotation of learning with a quiet, receptive spirit.' [45]

Gune, woman, is capable of meaning either 'female person' or 'wife'. Baldwin comments, 'It is clear that 2.11-15 refers to married women. [46] I should have thought one needs grounds for restricting the meaning to wives and do not see such in this passage. Knight observes, 'Contrariwise, the terms (i.e. for men and women) would seem to be meant more generally in verses 8-10 and, therefore, also in verses 11ff.' [47]

The meaning of *authentein,* to have authority over, has been much debated. George Knight points out that the rendering 'domineer', although inserted into Arndt-Gingrich's version of Bauer's lexicon, is not in the original German nor in the other translators or lexicographers [48]; and he summarises the evidence:

'The evaluation of all the documents surveyed places the meaning of the word 'authenteo' in the area of authority as a neutral concept. The most commonly suggested meaning is that of 'have authority over'. The word is not regarded as having any negative or pejorative overtone inherent within it such as is inherent in the rendering 'domineer'... This understanding of the term continues in the patristic evidence.' [49]

The primary confirmation of Knight's conclusion is surely the phrase 'in all submission' in v.11. It would seem that the rendering 'domineer' (and certainly 'be the source of') is unjustifiable for this New Testament *hapax legomenon* (= word that occurs only once); we must render it simply, 'to exercise authority'.

The tense of the infinitives *authentein* (to have authority over) and *didaskein* (to teach) is significant. Paul had a choice between the aorist infinitive, indicating a point or points in time (to have authority or speak even on individual occasions) and the present, indicating a continuum of time (to be in authority, or to be a speaker, on a steady continuous basis). The tense here is the present infinitive. Paul is not against women ever speaking or teaching, but in the comment of Wuest, 'The kind of teacher Paul has in mind is spoken of in Acts 13.1, 1 Corinthians 12.28f and Ephesians 4.11, as recognised by the Church as those having authority in the Church in matters of doctrine and interpretation.' [50] The passage harmonises exactly with the balance perceived in 1 Corinthians 11 and 14.

We are now in a better position to evaluate the three interpretations.

Paul says, 'A woman - let her learn with all submission. I do not permit a woman to teach, nor to have authority over a man.' Atkins reads this as, 'Come on, let women receive proper education; although I do not normally use them as teachers and leaders, you are free to.' I would observe:

First, Roman, Greek and Jewish societies at that time were all accustomed to women in leadership roles. Brooten has recently drawn attention to the inscriptional evidence for women as rulers of synagogues and exercising leadership in other ways in the Augustan period including well before Christ's coming [51]; and the Church of Scotland's Panel on Doctrine made the same point about Roman and Greek society. Thus Paul was not taking account of the proprieties of his own time but cutting somewhat across them. [52]

Secondly, *epitrepo,* permit, is a very strong word: 'do not *at all* allow such.' [53] Paul's comment is no disclaimer; rather the reverse. We cannot read it, with Atkins, 'It's not my normal practice just now (although I do sometimes, e.g. Phoebe) to use women in leadership positions.'

Thirdly, in not permitting women to have teaching ruling authority Paul is not, as Atkins claims, saying something merely personal and leaving others to choose their practice. He is speaking as an Apostle, an officer of Christ [54]. What Paul does not permit, Christ does not permit. Why, he goes on to explain.

Fourthly, Atkins is surely on shaky ground in her interpretation of verses 13,14. There is no hint that the Fall occurred because Adam (or God?) failed to educate Eve. Hurley's suggestion seems preferable. Eve took the lead, a position she had not been prepared for. Hence the Fall, and so 'I permit not a woman to teach/have authority over a man.' I conclude that there are several exegetical considerations which render Atkins's interpretation incredible.

What of Baldwin's position? We have already suggested reasons for reading *gune* as woman (not just wife) and preferring Hurley's overview of the passage to Baldwin's. Now compare these two clauses:

Text: *"I do not permit a woman to teach, nor to have authority."*

Baldwin: "It is inappropriate for wives, when they teach, to do so with a domineering attitude (although they may have whatever authority fits their standing in the congregation, as 1 Corinthians 11 allows)" [55].

The text indicates a situation in which women may not teach; Baldwin interprets this as saying in what attitude they are to do so. The text denies them a particular authority; Baldwin reads it as permitting it.

Exegesis alone, I believe, leads one to conclude that Hurley's summary rightly catches the thrust of these verses: 'The situation in view appears to be formal teaching in the assembly. Paul wants women to learn quietly and submissively and will not permit them to teach authoritatively. It is easy to see that the opposite of learning quietly and submissively is teaching verbally and with authority' [56].

The Kirk's Panel on Doctrine agreed. 1 Timothy 2.11-15 teaches from the principle of submission, they said, that it is unfitting for a woman to assume the authority in teaching in a Church. This teaching is based on Paul's interpretation of the creation story, not on social custom. 'On Paul's view this would exclude woman from an authoritative teaching ministry.' [57] But why just the Ministry? Both sides on the Panel on Doctrine agreed that according to Scripture, oversight (*episkope*, the work of a presbyter) should always be through men. When a court of the Church gives a ruling it is exercising what the New Testament would call a presbyteral role. 'It is precisely here that this text speaks to the role of women as elders. If any role in the church involves authority it is that of the elder' [58]. This is why so many have problems with the ordination of women to the Ministry and Eldership.

Ordination itself, hopefully, is not the issue at stake, but ordination *to the presbyterate*. The New Testament, many would argue, allows for different ordinations: a formal, perhaps permanent, setting apart to exercise a ministry of recognised standing for the sake of order and continuity; and a commissioning to given tasks, sometimes perhaps short-lived. The question is not 'Ordination?' but 'Ordination to what?' [59] It is to presbyteral work that the proscription of Scripture anent women's ministries applies.

'Ah, you're culturally conditioned,' said a feminist friend when I described where the evidence was taking me. Is this matter locked to a temporary situation? John Stott does not think so:

> 'The attempt has also been made by some to understand 1 Timothy 2.11ff as alluding to some particular, heretical, feminist movement. But I do not myself think it has been successful. The apostle's instruction sounds quite general: "A woman should learn in quietness and full submission. I do not permit a woman to teach or to have authority over a man; she must be silent".' [60]

Others have drawn a parallel between the abolition of male headship in the Church and the abolition of slavery. As the gospel contains the seeds of the abolition of slavery, it is argued, it contains also the seeds of a changed relationship between men and women in Christian service [61]. But there is no comparison between Scripture's treatments of the two subjects. In regard to slavery there are plain intimations of its future demise [62] whereas Scripture underlines the man-woman balance. Then consider

the basis of the proscription anent women's
headship.

Paul tells us his reasoning. His proscription is based
on the way God made things to be from the
beginning: '...not to teach or have authority over
men. For Adam was created first, and then Eve'
(v.12,13). It's Genesis ch.2 all over again; I do not
think it possible to gainsay that. But there is a second
reason: 'And it was not Adam who was deceived; it
was the woman who was deceived and broke God's
law' (v.14). Paul seeks to protect the Church from
being deceived in the kind of way which led to the
Fall. Neither of these reasons is time-locked; both fit
the creational pattern in his teaching on headship in
1 Corinthians 11.3ff and Ephesians 5.21ff.

1 Timothy 3.1-13
Verses 1-7 deal with the dignity of the presbyteral
office and the qualifications for it. Among them is
that a Bishop or Elder (the terms are
interchangeable: 'Bishop' indicates that his work is
oversight, 'Elder' his maturity) must be a 'one
woman male' (v.2); it might not prove anything but
fits in with the rest of the picture.

Verses 8-13 deal with the same matter in respect of
the Deacons with verse 11 dealing specifically with
'women likewise'. Who are they? There have been
many interpretations: Deacons' wives? Deaconesses?
Whatever the correct interpretation the principle is
that women have a ministry formally appointed to
diaconal not presbyteral work.

Women Elders in the Kirk?

Summary
The difference in role between men and women
belongs to the good order in the world as originally
made. Through the Fall this became domination but
this is not Christian headship. Through redemption
Christ reaffirmed and restored the created pattern of
headship. This is therefore not time-conditioned but
normative for the Church in all ages. Between the
Father and Christ, Christ and man, man and woman
one party is head.

All the most useful of Hayter's criteria for valid
exegesis [63] are satisfied by such a setting for headship.
Here is teaching which is Trinitarian, Christological
and based not on any proof-text or set of texts but
upon the whole pattern in creation and redemption.

The Gamaliel principle
In Acts five we read that Gamaliel warns his fellow
Sanhedrin members to wait and see if God will bless
this new movement Christianity, lest they find they
have been opposing God. If God continues to bless
the movement, he must be behind it. Similarly, it is
argued, if God blesses women's ministries - as he is
doing - he must be in favour of them.

It is a powerful point; but there are different ways of
exercising ministries. We see women ministers and
elders whose ministries are signally owned by God.
To break fellowship with them is unthinkable. Yet, as
indicated in the opening paragraphs of the chapter,
there are compelling reasons for seeking a pattern
which is faithful to the Scriptures.

The practical application of this teaching

We have seen the imperative to recognise and value women's gifts and ministries and to ensure acceptable channels for their exercise. We have seen that New Testament Christianity includes women speaking and praying during public worship. We have seen also that there is a church ruling-teaching authority which is not theirs. How are we to maintain this balance? John Stott suggests that women minister in team ministries and goes on:

'It is true that local church pastors are described as "over" the congregation in the Lord, and that the congregation is told "obey your leaders and submit to their authority"[64]. If all ordained Christian ministry inevitably has this flavour of authority and discipline about it, then indeed I think we would have to conclude that it is for men only. But if there are circumstances in which the pastoral care of people is a much more modest ministry, and the style of exercising it is humble, then no biblical principle is infringed if women are welcomed to share in it. I hope it is clear that the fundamental issue before the church is neither "priesthood", nor "ordination", but the degree of authority which necessarily inheres in the presbyterate. The practical problem, at least from an Anglican perspective, is whether women could be ordained to the presbyterate, and their ministry then restricted by licence to membership of a pastoral team. I still do not think it biblically appropriate for a woman to become a Rector or a Bishop.' [65]

David Watson took the same line, calling for women ministering but not with 'oversight authority':

> 'Women occupy (in the New Testament) a vital place in terms of Christian ministry...within the Christian Church the headship should ideally rest with the man, but when this is rightly understood and exercised, this simply gives the woman the protection or covering that she needs in (her) ministry: she is thereby given authority to act by the male leadership of the church... It would seem possible for a woman to be an elder, although coming under the primary authority of a presiding male elder... Could not a woman still be accepted as an "elder of women and children" within the congregation?... or given ready access to the meetings of elders.' [66]

I find Stott's and Watson's suggestions stimulating although Presbyterians hold dear the parity of ministers and the practicalities would need to be thought through. They would involve accepting elders' work as diaconal not presbyteral; we have seen the Biblical reasons for thinking otherwise.

Anne Atkins asks what women can do if the interpretation reached in this chapter is the right way to understand Scripture. We have not found this to be a problem in our own Church. Our full time Parish Assistant, a woman, was commissioned to her ministry by the laying on of hands and is a member of the Kirk Session; admittedly on the very rare occasions we come to vote she does not do so. Women speak at our Church meetings both midweek and on Sundays, lead in worship in a number of ways, take Bible studies, lead many outreach activities and chair committees. The policy of ordaining only men to the Presbyterate serves to identify, encourage and protect women's ministries.

Does our Lord Jesus want women elders and ministers? Women ministering, yes. Team ministry and women teaching in ways that do not infringe the biblical guidelines, yes. Women ministers and elders - his word seems to forbid it, unless Presbyterians can find a structure parallel to what John Stott suggests, guarding the issue of male headship.

NOTES

1. Text of letter from Pope John Paul II to the Archbishop of Canterbury in *The Times*, 28 April 1989, p. 6.
2. Editorial in *Free Church Record*, May 1988, p.108
3. For example, letter in *Life and Work*, April 1988 p.6 (Mrs R. Fraser).
4. So said Dr Andrew Herron in a letter to *Life and Work*, Feb. 1988, p.6.
5. G. Wainwright, *Christian Initiation*, Lutterworth, London 1969 p.80.
6. M. Hayter, *The New Eve in Christ*, SPCK, London 1987 p.84 quotes briefly from Gratian and Aquinas to illustrate the point; references on p.93 note 2.
7. A. Atkins, *Split Image*, Hodder, London 1987 p.42

8. P. Trible, *God and the rhetoric of sexuality*, p.195-223 Philadelphia 1978, p.99, quoted by Hayter op citp.100. I have been unable to obtain a copy of Trible.

9. J.B. Hurley in S. Lees ed.,*The Role of Women*, IVP, Leicester 1984 (hereafter called Hurley-Lees) p.135, cp. *New Bible Dictionary* , IVP, London 1962 art. "name" by A. Motyer.

10. Hurley-Lees op cit p.134.

11. Colossians 1.15-18.

12. 1 Cor.11.8-12

13. 1 Cor.11.3ff; Eph.5.21ff; 1 Tim 2.11ff.

14. Atkins, op cit, p.159-161

15. J.B. Hurley, *Man and Woman in Biblical Perspective*, IVP, Leicester 1981 (hereafter called Hurley *Man and Women*) p.31-57

16. Ibid p.34 quoting Deut. 21.13; 24.1; Is.54.5; Mal.2.11; cf Is.26.13

17. Numbers 30.3-16

18. 2 Kings 22.11-14

19. Prov.31.10ff; compare Atkins' nice exposition, op cit, p.71-97.

20. Hurley-Lees p.121-124. Compare Hurley, *Men and Women*, p.31-57.

21. Lev.7.31-36; Ex.28.1-5; Ex.29.passim; Ex.30.30-33; Num.1.47-53; Num.3.1-10.

22. Num.3.10.

23. See Lev.4.3ff, 13ff, 22ff, 27ff for the different treatment of priest, community, community leader and ordinary community member.

24. Hurley, *Men & Women*, p.56

25. John 4.27

26. e.g. Acts 1.14

27. Acts 2.16-21 and 21.9

28. Acts 18.26

29. Acts 20.17ff

30. J. Baldwin,*Women Likewise*, Falcon, London 1973 p.19.

31. Arndt & Gingrich, Gk-Eng *Lexicon* s.v.kephale. Also S. Bedale, 'The meaning of kephale in the Pauline epistles', *JTS* 5.1954, p.211-215. Although often quoted by "New View" protagonists Bedale's paper actually supports the conclusion I have come to.

32. Isaiah 9.13-15; Deut.28.13 and Judges 10.18 underline the point.

33. *Theological Dictionary of the NT,* Ed. Kittel,Trans. Bromiley, Eerdmans, Grand Rapids, 1964ff (Hereafter *TDNT*), s.v. kephale.

34. Hurley, *Men & Women,* p.166 shows this particularly clearly.

35. M.J. Williams, 'The Man-Woman Relationship in the NT', *Churchman* 91, 1977, p.33.

36. Compare Hurley, *Men and Women,* p.167 for the same point expressed slightly differently.

37. K. Barth, *Church Dogmatics*, III.1.183-195 and III.2.323f

38. G. Houston, *Prophecy Now,* IVP Leicester 1989 discusses the informal and occasional character of NT prophecy of this sort.

39. Reports to the General Assembly of the Church of Scotland, 1967, p.219-229

40. C.P. White, 'Women - their Role in the Church,' *Contactpoint* No.3, Glasgow, Spring 1978 p.17-21

41. 1 Thess. 5.12; cp Heb.13.17.

42. Luke 22.24-28

43. ATKINS: Anne Atkins, *Split Image,* Hodder, London 1987, p.114-124. BALDWIN: Joyce Baldwin, *Women Likewise,* Falcon, London, 1973, p.21,22. HURLEY: (a) James B Hurley in S. Lees ed., *The Role of Women,* IVP, Leicester,1984, p.131-137 (b) James B. Hurley, *Man & Woman in Biblical Perspective,* IVP, Leicester, 1981,

44. Hurley-Lees p.131

45. Ibid.

46. Baldwin op cit p.22.

47. G.W. Knight, *The NT Teaching on the Role Relationships of Men and Women*, Baker, Michigan, 1977 p.30.

48. G.W. Knight, (Authenteo in reference to Women in 1Tim.2.12), *'NTS'* 30,1984, p.143-157; also, P W Barnett *E.Q.* 61: 3, 1989, p. 225 - 238; L E Wilshire, 'The TLG Computer and Further Reference to Authenteo in 1Tim.2:12, *'NTS'* 34, 1988, p.120-134.

49. Ibid. Kroeger's thought otherwise (*'Women, Authority and the Bible'*, Marshalls, 1986), but see J. Panning's reply in *'Wisconsin Lutheran Quarterly'* ,78, 1981, p.185-191. Wilshire's evidence from the *Thesaurus Linguae Graecae*, (op. cit.) and the context of the verse support Knight and the position I have adopted.

50. K.S. Wuest, *The Pastoral Epistles in the Greek NT*, Eerdmans, Grand Rapids, 1954 p.49.

51. B.J. Brooten, *Women Leaders in the Ancient Synagogue*, Scholars Press, Chico California (Brown Judaic Studies No.36) 1982, passim.

52. Reports to the General Assembly 1967 p.219-229.

53. All nineteen occurrences of the word in the New Testament have the same issue of permission given or withheld on the highest authority. Moulton and Milligan *'The Vocabulary of the Greek NT'* Hodder, London, 1930 show the same meaning in the Greek of the time: "I now make this second order that the imperial moneys are not to be touched without leave": s.v. epitrepo.

54. Thus *TDNT* s.v. apostolos.

55. Baldwin op cit p.22.

56. Hurley-Lees op cit p. 131.

57. Reports to the General Assembly, 1967, p.219-229.

58. Hurley, *Man & Women*, p.132.

59. D. Watson, *I believe in the Church*, Hodder, London, 1978, p.288-291

60. J.R.W. Stott, *Issues Facing Christians Today*, Marshalls, Basingstoke 1984 p.251f.

61. C Craston, *Biblical Headship and the Ordination of Women*, Grove, Nottingham, 1986, p.18f; and many others.
62. e.g. Gal.3.28; Philemon (v.16 in context).
63. Hayter op cit p.146-168. But I cannot agree the New Testament has got it a bit wrong (p.166), even if Brunner thought so.
64. 1 Thess.5.12; Heb.13.17.
65. J.R.W. Stott op cit p.254.
66. D. Watson op cit p.277, 279, 282.

3

THE PRESENT SITUATION
by
Andrew T.B. McGowan

Introduction

There will be many people in the Church of Scotland
who feel that this book is unnecessary. The issue of
women in the eldership, they will say, is settled and
it is pointless and indeed unacceptable to raise the
matter again.

I quite understand that argument, and indeed I always
find it irritating when Presbytery reaches a decision
on some issue, and then someone raises the whole
matter again the next month! To go over the same
ground again wastes everyone's time.

Where the situation has changed, however, a re-
opening of the debate is justified. Even in a court of
law this is recognised. In the recent case of the
'Guildford Four' the defence counsel had to bring
'new evidence' before the case could be re-opened. I
want to suggest that certain 'new evidence', or rather
a 'changed situation', justifies re-opening the
discussion as to whether women should be elders in
the Church of Scotland.

The change about which I am speaking is not a change which concerns women elders themselves, it is a change in attitude by the Church towards those who do not feel able to participate in the ordination of women.

The best way to prove that a change has taken place is to give a 'before' and 'after' picture. First of all we must discover what was said when women were first enabled to become elders. In particular we must ask what was the 'intention' of the General Assembly in respect of those who were unhappy with the decision. Then we must look at certain recent statements and actions by officials and courts of the Church, which suggest that the attitude towards those unhappy with the decision has changed. Having done that I want us to reflect on the causes for the change which has occurred, and ask whether or not the change is acceptable.

Assurances

At the time when the decision was taken to permit women to be ordained to the eldership on the same terms and conditions as men, there was disquiet among those who disapproved of this proposal. Assurances were given, however, that this legislation would be 'permissive', and that no Kirk Session or congregation would be forced to do what they did not want to do.

The Rev. Dr W.R. Sanderson, in presenting the Supplementary Report of the Panel on Doctrine, assured members of the Assembly that,

'... this is only permissive legislation and eventually Kirk Sessions and Congregations will each be allowed to decide for themselves whether they want women Elders or not, it is only permissive legislation, it is not forcing women Elders on to congregations, it will be up to Kirk Sessions and Congregations to decide for themselves.... Each Kirk Session and Congregation would then have to make up their own minds whether they, in particular, were going to have women Elders. They would be allowed to have them, but they would have to make up their own minds if they were wanting them in their congregation.' [1]

This means, then, that when the General Assembly was asked to agree to the ordination of women to the eldership it was on the basis that the legislation was permissive and that no pressure would be brought to bear on those who were unwilling to have women as elders.

Now, having been a Presbyterian all my life, I realise that what was said by a Convener, or indeed by anyone else in the debate, is irrelevant in point of law. Only the minuted decision of the General Assembly, as enacted in the legislation, has any authority. Having said that, however, it must be recognised that many people voted for the legislation on the clear understanding that no-one would be forced to ordain women if they did not want to.

Women Elders in the Kirk?

This interpretation of the debate is reinforced by a letter in *Life & Work* from the Rev. Dr Andrew Herron, who expressed his concern that the assurances which he and others had given at the time of the debate were now being ignored, and the legislation was in danger of becoming prescriptive. Dr Herron wrote,

> 'I have a personal interest at stake here. When the 1966 Act lifting the ban on women elders came down under the Barrier Act I argued very strenuously with many who were bitterly opposed to it that they should vote in favour, because, I said, lifting the ban will not force you to have women if you don't want them, whereas by leaving the ban you are preventing those who do want women on their session from having them. The Act, I maintained, was permissive, not compulsive. It would seem I helped to get the Act passed under false pretences!' [2]

The words of the Convener, the testimony of Dr Herron, and discussions with some who were involved in the debate at the time, lead me to conclude as follows:

> The Church of Scotland decided that women should be ordained to the eldership on the same terms and conditions as men. In doing so, and recognising that opinion was divided on this contentious matter, it was the 'intention' of the General Assembly that the opponents of this legislation should be reassured as to their freedom

to choose for themselves whether or not this would apply to their congregations. In short, the legislation was understood to be permissive and not compulsive.

The Change

The change which has taken place, and which led Dr Herron to write his letter, has been gradual but significant. A number of Presbyteries now make the absence of women on a Kirk Session to be a matter worthy of comment. Some congregations have been told that they 'ought' to have women elders. Indeed, there have even been instances where severe pressure has been put on congregations to elect women to the Kirk Session with the suggestion being made that Presbytery would consider taking action if this were not done.

At a Quinquennial Visitation, one of the questions which must now be answered is whether the office-bearers are 'representative' of the congregation in terms of age, sex etc. Leaving aside for the moment the fact that elders are not 'representatives', but those in whom are recognised the God-given qualities described in 1 Timothy 3 there seems little doubt that the very existence of this question is related to the desire for every congregation to have women elders. Certainly I have heard a number of different ministers say that this is the way the question is being understood and used by visitation committees.

There has been, then, a gradual change from the old position, where the legislation was regarded as 'permissive' and it was left entirely to congregations and Kirk Sessions to decide as to whether or not they would have women elders, to a new position, where congregations which do not have women elders are made to feel that they are somehow in breach of Church law.

For a clear statement of the 'new' position we must turn to the Principal Clerk.

The Principal Clerk's Letter

The Rev. James Weatherhead, Principal Clerk to the General Assembly, last year sent out a 'Letter of Clarification' to all Presbyteries on the matter of women elders.

It was this letter which prompted Dr Herron to write in the terms quoted above, and which alerted many of us to the seriousness of our situation if the Clerk's interpretation of the law is accepted by the Church. Here is the full text of that letter:

> I have been asked for some clarification of the law of the Church on the question of women elders, in view of the fact that there are Kirk Sessions with no women in their membership.
>
> The operative clause of Act XXVIII, 1966, states: 'Women members of a congregation shall be eligible for election and admission as Elders on the same terms and conditions as men members of a congregation'.

In my opinion this can be construed only as follows:

1. Eligibility for the office of the eldership has been conferred by the General Assembly after reference to Presbyteries under the Barrier Act.

2. Any decision by a Kirk Session to the effect that women will not be considered for the eldership is a denial of the eligibility conferred by the General Assembly, and is therefore in breach of the law of the Church.

3. Any decision of a Kirk Session to exclude any particular woman from consideration for appointment to the eldership, simply on the grounds that she is a woman, is likewise in breach of the law of the Church.

4. For a Kirk Session to act contrary to the law, or for a minister or elder to seek to persuade a Kirk Session so to do, is a breach of the ordination vows taken by ministers and elders.

5. While the law stands as it is, there is no provision for conscientious objection to applying it. The General Assembly and the Presbyteries of the Church have considered the scriptural position in legislating, and their decision represents the 'conscientia' of the Church - ie. the collective and deliberate interpretation of scripture on the matter.

6. Individual views of scripture, and individual conscience, cannot prevail over the law of the Church. It is always open to anyone to exercise liberty of opinion (which is not liberty of practice, and not liberty to deny ordination vows) to the extent of seeking to persuade the Church to amend the law; but while the law stands as it is, it must be obeyed. [3]

Whatever else might be said about this letter, one thing is clear: a major change has taken place. From the position in 1965 where we were assured that it would be up to individual Kirk Sessions to decide whether or not to have women elders, we have now arrived at the position where it is illegal for a Kirk Session to decide to have no women elders (point 2 above).

This is assuming, of course, that the Principal Clerk is correct in his 'clarification'. Dr Herron believes that he is not correct, and many share that opinion.

Points 5 and 6 in the letter are substantially answered by what Ian Hamilton and David Young have written in their chapters, but let me respond to points 2, 3 and 4.

Point 2

The response to Mr Weatherhead on this particular point, namely, the right of a Kirk Session to decide that it will have no women elders, might go something like this:

We fully accept that women are eligible to serve as elders under the terms of the Act passed by the General Assembly, but the simple fact of eligibility places no obligation upon any Kirk Session to elect women to that office.

Surely this is self-evidently true? As a minister of the Church of Scotland I am eligible to be elected as Moderator of the General Assembly but, having several years to go before my fortieth birthday and being in many other ways unsuited for the position, I do not sit on the edge of my chair beside the telephone on the day the nomination committee meets! The simple fact of my eligibility is not sufficient to justify election. Let me put the issue more sharply: would it be illegal if the said nomination committee agreed to refuse consideration to anyone under the age of fifty, even although we are 'eligible'? Or, to give another example, is it illegal for a vacancy committee to refuse to consider Probationers even although they are eligible?

Point 3

Point 3 deals with the situation where a Kirk Session has not stated its opposition to women serving as elders, but at a meeting to consider one or more candidates someone objects to a particular candidate on the basis that she is a woman. Mr Weatherhead says that this is illegal.

In other words, during discussion at a Kirk Session meeting on possible elders, both men and women, the objections which can legally be raised against any of the candidates are objections on the basis of life, doctrine, ability, experience, spirituality, reliability or whatever - but simply to object to a possible candidate on the grounds that she is a woman is illegal. This seems to imply that those who oppose the ordination of women are not permitted to say so. This is confirmed when we turn to point 4.

Point 4

This point makes it clear that it would be illegal for a minister or an elder to seek to have a motion passed at Kirk Session precluding women from serving as elders in that particular congregation.

This, of course, raises a whole host of issues. It means that those of us who object to the ordination of women are not permitted to voice this opinion. What would happen if, during the meeting, someone asked me (as the 'Teaching Elder') for an interpretation of the passage in 1 Timothy which forbids women 'to teach or have authority'? [4] Am I supposed to ignore the question, or to give the 'collective and deliberate interpretation' of its meaning, or to tell the Kirk Session that I am not permitted to give my understanding of the text?

Many of us were deeply disturbed by the Principal Clerk's letter, partly because it presents us with a 'new' position in respect of the interpretation of Act XXVIII, 1966, and partly because it seems to represent a hardening of attitude against those of us who have genuine problems of conscience.

There are even some who fear that this is a specific attack on those of an 'evangelical' persuasion. It might reasonably be asked why this letter was not followed by similar letters of 'clarification' in respect of other aspects of Church law which are not universally obeyed. For example, it is well known that many ministers baptise the children of people who may be parishioners but are neither members nor adherents. Most Presbyteries 'smile' at this and take no action. Why, then, is there this 'hardening' on the issue of women's ordination? The 'new' position in respect of the interpretation of Act XXVIII, 1966, has also been seen in certain actions taken by Presbyteries. Let us consider two of these.

The St Andrews Case

The danger with the 'new' position is, of course, that we very quickly risk a situation where a minister is forced to leave the Church of Scotland because of his views on this matter. One recent case in the Church of Scotland highlights this danger, and indeed attracted the attention of the media, because that almost happened.

A minister in the Presbytery of St Andrews refused to ordain to the eldership a woman who had been chosen by his Kirk Session, because she was a woman. The Kirk Session appealed to the Presbytery. Presbytery instructed the minister to carry out the ordination. The minister appealed to the Synod.

Women Elders in the Kirk?

While that appeal was pending the minister left his congregation to take a position in a well-known Christian organisation.

Both those in favour of that minister's stand and those opposed to it are agreed that the law of the Church is so worded that the appeal (and the subsequent and final appeal to the General Assembly) was bound to fail. At that point, if the minister persisted in his refusal to ordain the woman, he would almost certainly have been deposed from the ministry.

This means that we now have a most unhappy situation prevailing in the Church of Scotland. There are ministers who deny the authority and inspiration of the Bible, deny the Virgin Birth, agree with the Bishop of Durham that Jesus Christ did not rise bodily from the dead, flout the law of the Church on baptism, and play fast and loose with their ordination vow vis a vis the Westminster Confession of Faith, and yet remain ministers of the Church in good standing. Indeed, the recent 'Quest' television series demonstrated that there are some ministers of the Church of Scotland who don't know what they believe!

On the other hand, despite this apparent 'freedom' and 'toleration', we find the Church of Scotland (or at least one Presbytery) taking action against a minister because he believes that the Bible is the Word of God written, believes that it has final authority on all matters, and disagrees with the General Assembly's interpretation of the passages which relate to the ordination of women.

Pre-Ordination Questions

Another disturbing event took place last summer at a Presbytery meeting when a call to a minister was being dealt with in the normal manner.

When the Moderator asked for any questions or objections, a member of Presbytery raised the matter of the minister's attitude to the ordination of women and asked the Convener of the Business Committee for clarification.

The Convener, having been forewarned of the question, said that he had telephoned all parties during the day, and indicated that he had received verbal assurances from the minister that he both knew and would obey the law of the Church anent women elders.

The questioner was unhappy with this and asked that a letter be sent to the minister inviting him to confirm these verbal assurances in writing. This was opposed, largely on the grounds that the assurances being sought were already covered by the ordination vows. On a vote being taken, however, the Presbytery agreed that the letter be sent.

It seems to me that this situation bears careful examination. Here was a minister who had successfully completed all his academic work. His probationary year had been sustained. He had received an unanimous call to a congregation, after making his views on the ordination of women very clear to them. They still wanted him. And yet a member of Presbytery felt it appropriate to demand written assurances against future conduct.

Has a Presbytery any right to demand of an ordinand any more than is laid down by the appropriate Act of Assembly? Can more questions be asked than those laid down in the formula to be signed?

That minister's views on this matter are precisely the same as my own, namely, that the ordination of women to the eldership is forbidden by the Bible. Both his congregation and mine accepted us knowing our views on this subject. What right does a Presbytery have to interfere where no law has been broken? Both that minister and myself know that if our Kirk Sessions elect a woman to the eldership then we shall have to carry out the ordination or leave or appeal. We know the law of the Church. But that surely should not prevent us from expressing our views and teaching them as we expound the Bible?

Conforming to the World

Having demonstrated that a change has taken place between 1965 and the present day, at least in interpretation and in attitude, we must now reflect a little upon why this is so, and question its legitimacy.

I believe that the answer lies in conformity to the world. One of the most serious problems facing

Christian theology today is the repeated and determined acceptance of secular presuppositions, and the refusal to decide issues by the criterion of Scripture. The Church in our day has tended to legitimise the current consensus (or even current 'fads') in society. The biblical injunction not to be conformed to the world but rather to be transformed by the renewal of the mind [5] has all but been forgotten. In short, theological issues are often decided purely on the basis of popular opinion.

Let us consider just two examples of this.

1.   Marriage and Divorce

There are many who would say that the Church's attitude to marriage and divorce has been 'watered down' because of pressure from popular opinion. Faced with an increasing divorce rate and the tendency of couples to live together outside of marriage, the Church has often been prepared to accommodate this spirit of the world. Many people have now stood in Church several times and taken the same vows, including the words, 'till death us do part,' with several different partners.

2.   Baptism

The General Assembly of the Church of Scotland in 1990 agreed to look again at its baptismal teaching and practice. In the public discussions leading up to this overture being remitted to the Panel on Doctrine there were a number of articles on the subject in *Ministers' Forum*. It became clear that the reason why so many Ministers want change is not fundamentally because of a dissatisfaction with the theology of baptism already held by the Church but rather because of the pressure we are under from popular opinion. In other words, we are constantly being asked to baptise children who quite simply ought not to be baptised, because their parents are not Christians and have no connection of any kind with the Christian Church! The Church is being asked to change its theology of baptism because of this pressure.

Now we have considered only two examples of this general trend and clearly others could have been mentioned. Also, much more could have been said about each of the examples given. The point has, however, been made. Instead of the Christian Church seeking to mould the consensus of thought and opinion in the world, we are often seen to be following meekly behind, allowing the world to set the agenda, and accepting the conclusions of secular humanism with hardly a whimper.

And that is precisely the situation in relation to the ordination of women. The world at large is increasingly bombarded with the message that women are, in every respect, equal to men. The Equal Opportunities Commission in this country was set up specifically to ensure that there is no 'discrimination' against women. This being the case, many people cannot understand why the Church should take a different approach. The idea that God might have given women a role within the family and within the Church which precludes leadership and teaching is regarded as outrageous.

If the Church is to be faithful to God it is necessary that issues be determined by the voice of God speaking in the Bible even if the conclusions which are then reached seem unacceptable to popular opinion in general and the consensus of secular humanism in particular. In short, we must say what the Bible says and not what the world says.

Conclusion

A major change has taken place in the Church of Scotland in the past 25 years. First, it was agreed that women 'could' be ordained to the eldership. Gradually this changed and we were told that they 'should' be ordained to the eldership. Now we are being told that they 'must' be ordained to the eldership.

Legislation which was originally permissive has become compulsive, so that those who are opposed to the ordination of women are being hounded and harassed. This is an intolerable situation. I believe that it will not be long before we have a case where a minister who is fully committed to both the Standard of the Church's faith (The Bible) and its principal Subordinate Standard (The Westminster Confession of Faith) is deposed from the ministry because of his views on the ordination of women.

Women Elders in the Kirk?

Are we prepared to accept such a situation? Or is it not time for the Church of Scotland to re-examine this matter in the light of the teaching of the Bible?

NOTES
1. Extract from the shorthand transcript of the proceedings of the General Assembly of the Church of Scotland, 1965.
2. February 1988 issue.
3. Sent to all Presbytery Clerks and dated July 1987.
4. 1 Timothy 2:12.
5. Romans 12:2.

4

WHERE WE STAND... and WHY
by
David A. Young

Introduction

It has been clearly demonstrated that the two pivotal issues on the question of women's ordination are the authority of Scripture and the right of conscience. We now explore these areas further. Let it be said at the outset that we do so not in order to disturb the peace of the Church. R.B. Kuiper has incisively commented:

> 'It is evident that we find it extremely difficult to carry on in love discussions of matters on which we differ. That ought not to be. Gossip, evil-speaking, back-biting and slander should not be heard among us. Let us firmly resolve to desist once and for all from the cruel pastime of setting up a straw man, knocking him down, tearing him to shreds, and withal leaving the impression that he who was demolished is some flesh-and-blood member of our Church. And let us beware of lightly accusing of lovelessness those of our number who vigorously oppose error and earnestly contend for the faith once for all delivered to the saints. Such judging is itself loveless in the extreme.' [1]

Rather, we do it to confront what we see to be a problem. A writer has said, 'Lack of controversy in the Church is often taken as a sign of spiritual maturity: but it can also be a sign of spiritual death.' [2] Painful as it may be, there are times when the nettle has to be grasped. It was no different in apostolic times. There were occasions when nothing short of outright confrontation was required. Perhaps no one ever valued the unity of the Church more than the Apostle Paul, but the very last thing that could be truthfully said of Paul was that he was a 'peace at any price' man who would go to any lengths to avoid conflict if he knew that basic, fundamental issues were at stake.

The Problem

In 1966 the General Assembly passed the Act which states: 'Women members of a congregation shall be eligible for election and admission as Elders on the same terms and conditions as men members of a congregation'. [3] As Andrew McGowan has shown, this decision of the General Assembly was taken on the clear understanding that the legislation being sought was only permissive. [4]

It is very important to understand this. Many elders and ministers who may well have had grave reservations on the matter, were urged to vote in favour so that those who wanted women on their Sessions would not be prevented from so having. And many men have no doubt entered into the ministry of our Church on this understanding of the legislation.

In recent days, however, as we have seen, the law has been interpreted by the Principal Clerk in such a way as to suggest that it is indeed compulsive and not permissive. [5]

We have been informed that: any decision by a Kirk Session that women will not be considered for the eldership is in breach of the law; for a Kirk Session to act contrary to the law is a breach of ordination vows; there is no provision for conscientious objection to applying it; individual views of Scripture and an individual conscience cannot prevail over the law of the Church. While the law stands as it is, it must be obeyed.

On the basis of this interpretation, many of us find that such a law is quite unacceptable, and we do so for two reasons. First, because we believe that while the issue of women's ordination is the one at stake, the real issue is a far bigger one, it is none other than the authority of the Bible. Second, because we believe that for the General Assembly of any Christian Church to place a man into a situation which would require him to act against his conscience, is to do violence to one of the most basic truths taught in the Scriptures, as well as one of the most glorious blessings of the Reformation, namely, religious freedom. 'God alone is Lord of the conscience'. [6] This is an inalienable and fundamental right of every Christian believer. Men have absolutely no rights over our minds or over our consciences.

Women Elders in the Kirk?

What the Authority of Scripture means in Practice

Some of us are opposed to the ordination of women, for the very same reason that we are opposed to the ordination of certain men, and that is, because of Scripture. We understand that there can be no place for the ordination of women in the Church either as elders or ministers because we believe God in his Word does not allow it.

Now many are not troubled by this issue, and we fully recognise that there are genuine differences of opinion. For our part we can only say what we believe to be right, and seek an honest discussion. We must respect one another, even although we may disagree with one another.

We are saying, therefore, that this is our conviction. It must also be stressed that there is no suggestion here that women are inferior to men. Rather, we believe that God has ordained a certain order in his Church such that only men should hold positions of authority and teaching. 'In the Church, redemption in Christ gives men and women an equal share in the blessings of salvation; nevertheless, some governing and teaching roles within the Church are restricted to men.' [7] We believe that God is perfectly clear about that in his Word and we are bound by that Word of God. For us, the scriptural pronouncement is final: it is the end of all strife and controversy. We refuse to ordain women to the office of elder or minister, not because we wish to keep it as some kind of male preserve, but because God's Word appears to us clearly to debar women from the office of teaching and rule in the Church.

We regard the ordination of women as being contrary to Scripture and do not believe the Church has clearly demonstrated from the Scriptures that we are in error. Indeed, it is probably not without significance that we read in the report of the Committee on "The Role of Men and Women in Church and Society," which deals specifically with the 'official position of the Church', as follows:

> 'It is now part of the Church's teaching that the exercise by women of the Eldership and the Ordained Ministry is agreeable to the Word of God and the fundamental doctrines of the Christian faith.' [8]

The next part, however, is really most revealing:

> 'It is important to take note that the main argument which led to the Church's change of attitude was the recognition that in the intervening years there had been developments both in the Church and in society which led to new understandings both of scripture and of the Church's traditions.'

In other words, the opening of the eldership and ministry to women was due to the Church changing its mind about the teaching of the Scriptures on the roles of men and women, because society had changed its mind about them, and that the Church 'has the task of theologising the new developments in society'. And that is precisely what many of us feared the argument to be based upon: certainly not on the teaching of the Scriptures.

What Liberty of Conscience means in Practice

A very real part of the difficulty in the discussion of the issue of women's ordination is the danger of getting caught up with the minutiae, and forgetting that a major issue that has to be faced here is religious freedom, or liberty of conscience. Notice that we do not say 'licence'. We do not believe that man has an absolute and unlimited right to believe and to act simply as his conscience dictates. Liberty of conscience is always limited by the authority of God.

A.H. Rehwinkel has defined conscience as,

> '...that faculty by which one distinguishes between the morally right and wrong, which urges one to do that which he recognises to be right and restrains him from doing that which he recognises to be wrong, which passes judgement on his acts and executes that judgement within his soul.' [9]

And the place of conscience is carefully defined in our own Subordinate Standards, in Chapters 31:4 and 20:2:

> 'Since apostolic times all Synods and Councils whether general or local, may make mistakes, and many have. Consequently, Synods and Councils are not to be made a final authority in questions of

faith and living, but are to be used as an aid to both.'

'God alone is Lord of the conscience and has left it free from the doctrines and commandments of men which are in any way contrary to or different from his Word in matters of faith or worship. And so, believing any such teachings or obeying any such commandments of men for conscience's sake actually betrays true freedom of conscience. Requiring implicit or absolute, blind obedience also destroys freedom of conscience as well as the free use of reason.' [10]

What we are saying then is this: not only do we genuinely believe that the decision of the General Assembly to open the eldership and ministry to women was in error; but we are also claiming the *right* so to believe.

Others may, and do, believe differently. That is not the issue. They are not being denied their rights. But there is a significant number of ministers and elders within the Kirk whose love for the Kirk and whose loyalty to the courts of the Kirk is being seriously threatened by their primary love and loyalty to God and their necessary obedience to his voice speaking in Scripture. Herein lies the heart of the matter. We are opposed to the ordination of women because of Scripture. We believe that we may not ordain women to the office of teaching or ruling elder because God, in his Word, does not allow it. In fact, we believe the Bible has some of the profoundest things to say against the idea of women's leadership. And the question that really needs to be answered is this: who has the right to tell us that we believe otherwise? Our congregations? The Kirk Session? The Presbytery? The Principal Clerk? The Moderator? An Assembly Committee? The General Assembly?

We think not. No man has that right. No Church has that right. There is no infallible man. There is no infallible Church. There is no General Assembly or any other group of Church leaders whose pronouncements about Scripture are always to be trusted. Scripture judges the Church, not vice versa. Our loyalty must be first of all to God's Word, and then to the Church only so far as we find that Church faithful to God's Word. A Christian is one who has been set free by Christ to follow God's Word. And that is why we are bound to disagree with, and to dissent from, the decisions of ministers and elders when we believe that they misunderstand or misinterpret God's Word. That is why, ultimately, when an Assembly issues any decree or order which conflicts with the Word of God, it must be disobeyed.

The Church has no right to make laws of its own that contradict or even augment the Law of God. A Church may neither allow what God forbids, nor forbid what God allows. And yet, we have been informed that we have 'liberty of conscience' - we may believe what we like as regards the teaching of Scripture; but we do not have 'liberty of practice' - we may not act in accordance with what we believe.

Now no matter how valid that argument may be in the minds of our legal profession, might we suggest respectfully, that theologically such a notion is not tenable.

In his excellent exposition of the Westminster Confession of Faith, Robert Shaw has written,

> 'The conscience in all matters of faith and duty is subject to the authority of God alone and entirely free from subjection to the traditions and commandments of men. To believe any doctrine, or obey any commandment, contrary to, or beside the Word of God, out of submission to human authority, is to betray true liberty of conscience. And be the power and authority whose it will - be it that of a Magistrate or a Minister - of a husband, a master, or a parent - that would require an implicit faith and an absolute blind conscience, it would destroy liberty of conscience.' [11]

We need to ask, therefore, by what authority did the General Assembly of 1966 pass an Act which would ultimately bind the conscience of its elders and ministers? There is something very far wrong when any minister of the gospel declines to do what he finds contrary to Scripture, and is told by a Presbytery or a General Assembly that he has no choice but to act against his conscience. Such a requirement must, surely, be ultra vires. Such a Church Court has set itself above the standards it claims to hold.

We are, after all, a Presbyterian Church, and it is of the essence of Presbyterian Church government that in matters on which the Scriptures are clear, we are bound by the Scriptures; that in areas where the Scriptures are not clear, we must exercise toleration; and that in matters on which the Scriptures are silent, we have absolute freedom.

This does not preclude the Church from trying to establish a policy in regard to specific issues, but no Reformed Church must compel those who genuinely disagree on biblical and conscientious grounds to comply with a majority decision of one particular General Assembly.

Each individual Christian has a duty to judge for himself, by the Word of God, whether something is God's truth, or not. We are urged by the Apostle Paul to "test all things". [12] Is a certain thing contrary to what God has made known? Then 'hold off'. If it is not, then 'hold on' to it. Samuel Bolton has written,

> 'It is my exhortation therefore to all Christians to maintain their Christian freedom by constant watchfulness. You must not be tempted or threatened out of it; you must not be bribed or frightened out of it; you must not let either force or fraud rob you of it. To what purpose is it to maintain against those who are the open enemies of it, and against others who would take it from us, and yet give it up to them by our own hands, to them perhaps who do not seek it from us?

Nothing is more unusual. We must therefore beware. We must not give up ourselves to the opinion of other men, though they be never so learned, never so holy, merely because it is their opinion. The apostle directs us to try all things and to hold fast that which is good.' [13]

It is no part of Christian simplicity to be credulous.

There is something deeply disturbing about this notion that ministers owe implicit obedience to the General Assembly, that while Scripture is our rule, the Church is to be the interpreter of what the rule means. In a previous generation, ministers and elders owed their allegiance to the Word of God, to the Standards of the Church, and to the General Assembly in that order. Now, we are told, our primary allegiance is to the General Assembly.

The General Assembly, however, is not infallible.

'The pronouncements of the Presbytery or Synod or Assembly are not necessarily the voice of God... Synods and councils may err, and many have erred. It is this that precludes them from being the rule of faith or practice. Their design is to be a help, and they must be tested by the teaching of Scripture. The touchstone is always, 'What saith the Scriptures?' If they are in line with the teaching of the Scriptures, they are to be received; if they are not, they are not to be received.' [14]

Women Elders in the Kirk?

It is precisely because 'God alone is Lord of the conscience' that the question put to ministers at ordination is: 'Do you promise to be subject in the Lord to this Presbytery and to the superior courts of the Church?' [15] That phrase, 'in the Lord' gives a man liberty of conscience. It allows a minister 'to obey God rather than men', should the Presbytery or Assembly require him to act against his conscience. 'In all of life Christ is the supreme authority and guide for men and women, so that no earthly submission - domestic, religious or civil - ever implies a mandate to follow a human authority into sin.' [16] We simply cannot assent to the message, in the Principal Clerk's letter referred to above, that 'For a Kirk Session to act contrary to the law, or for a Minister or Elder to seek to persuade a Kirk Session so to do, is a breach of the ordination vows taken by Ministers and Elders'. If that is the case, then we are subject to the courts of the Church 'simpliciter' and not 'in the Lord'.

For example, what if a minister in expounding 1 Timothy 3 tells his people that an elder must be a man. And the same minister, a week later, finds himself having to participate in the ordination of a woman because he is not at liberty to practise what he believes. What would our people make of that? What would they think? Such a minister would not have an ounce of credibility left to his name. Surely every minister and elder has the right - given him in his ordination vows - to refuse to participate in any ceremony which he believes to be contrary to the Word of God.

The enormous importance and implications which follow, of a man's freedom of conscience, cannot be overstated. It was precisely the existential accommodation of objective Scripture to the mind and will of the Church that Martin Luther so opposed at Worms and, indeed, throughout the greater part of his life. Luther was faced with the demand of the Church to abandon his conscience for the sake of peace and unity. He replied,

> 'Unless I am convicted by Scripture and plain reason - I do not accept the authority of Popes and Councils, for they have contradicted each other - my conscience is captive to the Word of God. I cannot and will not recant anything, for to go against conscience is neither right nor safe. God help me. Amen.' [17]

And this is the position of all those within the Kirk who view the 1966 Act, and the Principal Clerk's interpretation of that Act, with such grave concern. They will have to say to their Presbyteries, 'My conscience is captive to the Word of God... to go against conscience is neither right nor safe.' They will refuse to accept that ministers and elders have 'liberty of conscience' with respect to the ordination of women, but not 'liberty of practice'.

The Need for Amendment

Apart from the obvious and fundamental 'wrongs' already discussed, there are a number of other difficulties apparent, of which we would mention:

1.   *The obscurity of the Act.* What is it really saying? If ministers and elders refuse to comply, on the ground of conscience, are they going to be asked to resign?

2.   *The restriction being imposed.* Ministers are no longer free to move to certain charges, they are locked into their present situations and cannot move. Congregations, too, are being limited in their freedom to call the man of their choosing and that, surely, is one of the most deeply cherished privileges of Presbyterianism.

3.   *The encouragement to sin.* Every man ought to be his own judge, under God, on every question as to whether a Church law is biblical or not, and no court of the Church should decide for him. But our Church is binding men to do what Scripture does not bind them to do - and to do it in an area where reasonable and godly men differ so very widely. The danger is that men who believe in the authority of Scripture and freedom of conscience 'will do it anyway' because the General Assembly of the Church says so.

4.   *The debarring of entry.* The Church of Scotland is proud of its theological breadth - there are men whose beliefs range across a wide spectrum.

That has long been a feature of the Kirk's ministry. But this law, as it stands, is going to effectively deny certain men the opportunity to minister. Whether the Church likes it or not, we have known immense blessing in past days under the ministries of some of the godliest of men who have stood, resolutely, for the preaching of the Word of God, and the application of Biblical principles in all matters of life and doctrine - men like the Bonars, Chalmers, McCheyne, Melville, Rutherford - to name but a few, and to say nothing of similar men in our present day. In the light of this present law, and in view of their own convictions about the ordination of women to the ruling and teaching eldership, it would simply not be possible for men like this, consistently and with a clear conscience, to apply to be accredited as suitable candidates for ministry in the Kirk.

Baptism & Marriage

In the course of this debate we are constantly being told two things: first, Presbytery cannot allow ministers to break the law of the Church; and second, you cannot have a law with a 'conscience clause'. But is this true?

It seems that there are two questions which when answered, shed considerable doubt on these propositions. First, is there precedent for ministers being permitted to break a law with which they do not agree? And second, is there precedent for a law with a conscience clause?

97

Women Elders in the Kirk?

The first question can be answered in one word: Baptism. The 1963 Act anent Baptism is a classic example of a Church law being openly flouted by ministers who have no scruples about the indiscriminate administration of the Sacrament of Baptism, despite regulations which are very clear. Yet it is rare for a Presbytery to take any action against such ministers. Indeed, in a recent obituary in *Life & Work*, a glowing tribute was paid to a minister who, 'as a matter of principle "would christen or marry anyone who asked".' Not only is the law breached, but everyone knows that it is breached, and it is even considered to be an appropriate word of commendation!

The second question can be answered in relation to the remarriage of divorced people. On the 'remarriage of Divorced Persons' the Church has expressed its mind as follows: 'A Minister shall not be required to solemnise a re-marriage against his conscience.' [18]

In other words, a minister may consider that the grounds on which a divorce has been granted, while perfectly legal, do not have a biblical warrant, and so refuse to officiate at the wedding. By permitting this course of action the Church recognises that a Minister must not be required to act against his conscience. Is there not some way forward on the basis of these examples of precedent?

A Call For Action

Here, as in most areas of disagreement, it is not always easy to know how to act in a manner consistent with one's views, and particularly how to hold together one's convictions along with the very important principle of the peace and unity of the Church. On the one hand, we believe ourselves to be conscience-bound not to participate in the ordination of women; and on the other hand, as stated at the very outset, we continue to love and to hold in proper honour those whose convictions and/or practice may be very different from ours.

Very broadly speaking, there are two categories of men involved. There are those seeking admission to the Church of Scotland now, that is, since the 1966 Act; and there are those who were already in the service of the Church prior to 1966 or who, at the time of ordination since 1966, came in in good faith, with every reason to believe that the present legislation was only permissive and, therefore, they would never be forced to ordain women.

In respect of the first category it must surely be pointed out that those seeking entry to the ministry of the Church of Scotland are responsible for informing themselves of the terms of ordination and the enacted laws of the Church. [19] Seeking admission now will imply that a man has approved those conditions and will subscribe to them unless, afterwards, he recognises them to be unbiblical and, as such, cannot, in good conscience, submit to them. But such a sensitive conscience will then be resolved - not by disobedience to the previously agreed conditions - but by either withdrawing from the denomination whose laws he had believed biblical, or by seeking to amend the rules he once agreed, but now finds unbiblical. Because this is a right every minister has. He has every right, for example, in the particular area of this present discussion, to test the law of the Church, to see whether it means that he must proceed to ordain women against his conscience and, if necessary, then to move and to argue for a change through the proper channels provided by the Church's constitution.

Those in the second category have a much stronger position. They were ordained into a Church which did not permit women to serve as ministers or elders, and they voted against the 1966 Act. They have every right to demand that the Church respects their conscience on this matter. They have not changed, the Church has changed.

Available Options

Having said that, however, it does not seem that there are too many options available to us. Among them there are the obvious:

1. *Resign.* Secede from the denomination.

2. *Sin.* Do what one believes to be wrong. After all 'the General Assembly says it' or 'the Presbytery has instructed it' or 'everyone else is doing it'. In other words, obey man rather than God.

3.   *Disobey.*   Defy the law of the Church, in the name of the Holy Spirit who speaks through the Scriptures, and make the Church responsible - and answerable - for severing our pastoral tie.

4.   *Stand firm.*   Remain where we are and seek reform through the courts of the Church. The first of these options we would consider only as a last resort. The second we would resist with every fibre of our being. After all, it is not we who have changed our position. Precisely where we stand and why is the substance of this publication. Many of us were born and reared within the Church of our fathers; to say it is dear to us is a shocking understatement. We love our Kirk and will serve her with that 'zeal for the glory of God, love to the Lord Jesus Christ, and a desire for the salvation of men' [20] as promised. Timothy Dwight says it for us in his great hymn:

> I love Thy church, O God:
> Her walls before Thee stand,
> Dear as the apple of Thine eye,
> And graven on Thy hand.
> For her my tears shall fall,
> For her my prayers ascend,
> To her my cares and toils be given,
> Till toils and cares shall end. [21]

And we love our people. Some of us have served in our charges over many years and have known the thrill and the unspeakable privilege of that 'Pastoral tie' which has bound our hearts with theirs in that

Women Elders in the Kirk?

Christian love which is not of this world; and which constrains us, as parish ministers, to do our utmost and to give our all for them. We would not see that tie severed lightly. And therefore we will never leave our denomination, nor our people - as long as it is possible to remain without compromising obedience to Christ - for which our people would respect us.

The third option, hopefully, we will not have to face. And that leaves the fourth. We must remain and seek to work for the reform of the law through the proper channels. This, in effect, means that we will make an earnest plea for the law to be amended. We are told that, 'while the law stands as it is, there is no provision for conscientious objection to applying it'. We believe that the formulation of such provision is well within the reach of those whose task it is to draw up our Church laws - some of the most able legal minds in our land are office bearers in the Kirk.

The Anglican Church in Canada managed it. In 1975 the General Synod passed the resolution,

> 'that it would be appropriate for women qualified for the priesthood to be ordained at the discretion of diocesan bishops acting within the normal procedures of their own jurisdictions and in consultation with the House of Bishops.' [22]

Subsequently the same Synod passed what has come to be known as 'the Conscience Clause':

> 'Be it resolved that no bishop, priest, deacon or lay person including postulants for ordination of

the Anglican Church of Canada should be penalized in any manner, nor suffer any canonical disabilities, nor be forced into positions which violate or coerce his or her conscience as a result of General Synod's action in affirming the principle of the ordination of women to the priesthood and requests those who have authority in this matter to act upon the principle set out above.' [23]

True, we are not Anglicans, and neither are we unaware of the complexities involved in reaching a solution. One area of particular difficulty will no doubt be where a minister finds his conscience interfering with the rights and, presumably, the consciences of the members of his Kirk Session who have chosen a woman to be one of their number. If some understanding is to be reached, it may very well be that that minister decides either to move to some other charge where his conscientious convictions will be more widely shared; or he agrees to another minister coming in to carry out the ordination.

Much in the way of discussion will require to take place. Nevertheless, some of us genuinely believe that there is no warrant in Scripture for women to be ordained. This is a matter of conscience. To ordain would violate our conscience. This is our position. There is no suggestion that it is the only position. But it is ours; and that is why we must seek, on the grounds of conscience, to be excused participation in the ordination of women.

NOTES

1. Quoted by George C. Fuller and Samuel T. Logan Jr., in *Innerancy and Hermeneutic,* edited by Harvie M. Conn (Baker Book House, 1988) p.237.

2. *The Bulwark* (Scottish Reformation Society, Edinburgh) March/April 1989.

3. The General Assembly of the Church of Scotland, 1966, Act XXVIII.

4. Extracts from the shorthand transcript of the General Assembly, 1965.

5. Letter of "clarification of the law of the Church on the position of women elders" by the Principal Clerk, June 1987.

6. *The Westminster Confession of Faith,* Chapter 20:2.

7. Council on Biblical Manhood and Womanhood. The Danvers Statement. Affirmation 6.

8. The Report of the Committee on the Role of Men and Women in Church and Society, 1978. Section 17, page 5.

9. 'Conscience' in *Evangelical Dictionary of Theology,* edited by Walter A. Elwell (Baker Book House, 1984) p.267.

10. *The Westminster Confession of Faith.* A new edition. Edited by Douglas Kelly, Hugh McClure and Philip B. Rollinson (The Attic Press, 1981).

11. *The Reformed Faith* by Robert Shaw (Christian Focus Publications, 1974) p.205.

12. 1 Thessalonians 5:21,22

13. *The True Bounds of Christian Freedom* by Samuel Bolton (Banner of Truth Trust, 1964) p.221.

14. *The Westminster Confession of Faith: An Exposition* by James Philip (Didasko Press, 1984) Vol.2, p. 166.

15. *Ordinal and Service Book* of the Church of Scotland (Oxford University Press, 1962) p.18.

16. Council on Biblical Manhood and Womanhood. The Danvers Statement. Affirmation 7.

17. *Here I Stand* by Martin Luther edited by Roland Bainton (Lion Publishing) p.185.
18. Act of the General Assembly of the Church of Scotland anent "Re-marriage of divorced persons" 1959, XXVI, paragraph 6.
19. See the argument in *Discussions: Evangelical and Theological 2* by R.L. Dabney (Banner of Truth Trust, 1967) pp.584ff.
20. *Ordinal and Service Book* of the Church of Scotland (Oxford University Press, 1962) p.18.
21. Hymn Number 347, written by Timothy Dwight, in *Christian Hymns* (Evangelical Movement of Wales, 1978).
22. "Report of the Task Force on Liberty of Conscience as it Pertains to the Ordination of Women with Supportive Material" as appointed by the Presbyterian Church in Canada. 1981 p.26.
23. ibid.

CONCLUSION

Summary
Let me begin by summing up what I believe to be the main thrust of this book.

The Bible is the Word of God, and every aspect of the life and work of the Church must, therefore, be in accordance with the Bible. We believe that in respect of the ordination of women to the eldership the Church of Scotland is out of step with what the Bible teaches.

The position which the Church currently holds is that women may be ordained as elders. This is a position which was only formulated about twenty five years ago. There are many men within the ministry of the Church who were ordained before that change took place, and who disagree with the change. It is the Church which has changed its mind and not them. They should not be penalised.

A further change has taken place since then, namely in the attitude towards those who do not believe in the ordination of women. Legislation which was originally permissive is in danger of becoming

107

compulsive. The effect of this is to create the possibility of someone being deposed from the ministry for refusing to participate in the ordination of women. This particularly affects those who have become ministers since 1966, because they knew the law (or ought to have done).

We do not believe that the situation is hopeless. It seems to us that the Church must seek a way out of this impasse. We have sometimes been told that Church law must be obeyed without any possibility of accomodation, and that there cannot be a conscience clause in respect of a law. In response to this we would cite the law anent baptism, which is not universally obeyed, and the law anent the remarriage of divorced persons, which has a conscience clause. We are not suggesting that either of these examples provides a formula for solving this present difficulty but they at least demonstrate that flexibility can, and does already, exist within Church law.

The Irish Presbyterians

One striking example of how this might be done has recently been provided by the Presbyterians in Ireland.

The Presbyterian Church in Ireland, like the Church of Scotland, has ruled that women may be ordained as elders and ministers on the same terms and conditions as men. Apart from the fact that elders are ordained by Presbytery rather than by the minister and the Kirk Session of the congregation to which they belong, the law of that Church on the issue of women's ordination is the same as that of the Church of Scotland.

That denomination, however, has already recognised the problem to which this book is trying to draw attention, and steps have been taken to remedy the situation.

At the 1989 General Assembly of the Presbyterian Church in Ireland, a petition was brought, signed by 110 ministers, asking that the conscience of those who felt unable to ordain women should be respected.

At the 1990 General Assembly the Judicial Commission brought forward a series of guidelines on the matter which were subsequently approved by the Assembly. There are two points in these guidelines which merit particular attention when thinking about our parallel situation in the Church of Scotland.

First, it was agreed that no candidate for ordination should be rejected because he did not share the theology which would permit women to be ordained. That is to say, a candidate who is opposed to women's ordination is not thereby precluded from admission to the denomination as a minister.

Second, and more significantly, the following guideline:

'Those with personal conscientious objections to participation in a particular service have the freedom to decline for themselves but not to dictate or veto who may be invited by the appropriate Church court or authority.'

Now this is a most significant development. It proves that a 'conscience clause' can be applied to Church law as it relates to the ordination of women. It also demonstrates that the issue is a significant one, affecting other Presbyterian denominations and not simply the Church of Scotland. Finally, it establishes beyond doubt that a denomination, when faced with an issue such as this, can and should act to protect the Bible-instructed conscience of its ministers.

The Way Ahead

What, then, is the way ahead? David Young has outlined some of the options which are open to us, and no doubt there are others. The real issue at stake is this: does the Church of Scotland really want to seek for a solution?

There are, undoubtedly, some who would like those of us who are opposed to the ordination of women simply to leave the denomination. That cannot be the answer. We are ministers of the Church of Scotland, and have no desire to be anything else. It would be quite wrong for us to concede the situation, walk away from the issue, and simply leave the denomination.

The way forward must be for those who are on

opposite sides of the fence to meet and to talk. If those of us who feel strongly about the matter were to sit down and discuss the various options with the Principal Clerk and others, then surely it would be possible to resolve the situation before someone ends up in front of the Judicial Commission?

It would be invidious to mention names, but there are a number of senior ministers who have the respect of both sides in this dispute and who could perhaps create a forum to examine the alternatives which are open to the Church.

We would gladly accept an invitation to such a forum. No sensible person wants another 'Disruption', nor even the departure of a significant number of evangelicals from the Church of Scotland. Let us do all that we can to prevent this possibility by seeking, under God, to find a solution.

This must not be taken to mean, however, that we are content to be accommodated, or to become a 'party' within the Church. Our ultimate aim is to see the Church of Scotland reformed and renewed according to the teaching of the Bible.